EXPERIMENTS IN ARTIFICIAL NEURAL NETWORKS

Advanced Technology Series

Experiments with EPROMS
By Dave Prochnow
Edited by Lisa A. Doyle

Experiments in
Artificial Neural Networks
By Ed Rietman
Edited by David Gauthier

EXPERIMENTS IN ARTIFICIAL NEURAL NETWORKS

Ed Rietman

TAB BOOKS Inc.
Blue Ridge Summit, PA

To all those who recognize and encourage creativity.

FIRST EDITION
SECOND PRINTING

Library of Congress Cataloging in Publication Data

Rietman, Ed.
Experiments in artificial neural networks / by Ed Rietman.
    p. cm.
    Bibliography: p.
    Includes index.
    ISBN 0-8306-0237-2   ISBN 0-8306-9337-8 (pbk.)
    1. Parallel processing (Electronic computers) 2. Neural
circuitry. 3. Artificial intelligence. 4. Digital computer
                simulation. I. Title.
QA76.5.R484   1988   88-1510
006.3—dc 19   CIP

TAB BOOKS Inc. offers software for
sale. For information and a catalog,
please contact TAB Software Department,
Blue Ridge Summit, PA 17294-0850.

Questions regarding the content of this book
should be addressed to:

Reader Inquiry Branch
TAB BOOKS Inc.
Blue Ridge Summit, PA 17294-0214

Contents

Experiments in Artificial Neural Networks

List of Projects

Project 1: Two-Processor Flip-Flop
Project 2: An Interfaceable N-Flop Circuit
Project 3: Electronic Neural Computer

Program List

Computer programs for the book *Experiments in Artificial Neural Networks*.

PROGRAMS FOR CHAPTER 3

NEURON4P
NEURON5P
NEURON6P
NEURON8P
HEBB2P
HEBB3P

PROGRAMS FOR CHAPTER 4

NETWORKP

All programs are written on an AT&T 6300 (an IBM clone), MS-DOS and GWBASIC.

Acknowledgments

This book is a zeroth level introduction to neural networking. It is a result of my efforts as a computer hacker and is therefore intended for hackers and experimenters. However, scientists and students looking for a good starting-level book might also find Chapter 2 most useful. I have not attempted to include the latest of computer models nor do I discuss the latest hardware. Specifically discussed in this book are the Hopfield network, Hebb learning rule, and content-addressable memories. These are the starting points for all the advanced theories covered in research journals.

There are many people I would like to thank. Cody Stumpo for putting up with my low blood sugar. Peter Littlewood for reviewing Chapters 2, 3, and 4. Thanks to Wayne Hubbard for helpful conversations and long phone calls. I would like to also thank Ed Spencer, David Tank, David Kleinfeld, and John Hopfield for helpful conversations. I thank Lynn Jelinski for enthusiastic support.

I thank my best friend, my lover, my editor, my wife—Suzanne Harvey.

Introduction

Parallel distributed processing is a model for cognition and a very efficient method for processing of information. The processing element can be a 32-bit processor, a microcomputer linked through a connection network, or a simple threshold logic device, such as a neuron. This book is an introduction to parallel distributed processing with threshold logic devices. I wrote the book primarily to clarify my thinking about artificial neural networks and to introduce the elementary theory of threshold logic processing through computer models and hardware experiments.

In Chapter 2, I assume the reader has some background in algebra. I then develop the methods of vector and matrix algebra, using examples from parallel distributed processing. For Chapter 3 you will need little more than a knowledge of how to use a PC. The programs are written for an IBM PC, running BASIC, but should run on any system using BASIC. For large simulations, the processing time can be long, and a compiled BASIC can be used. I use a compiled BASIC with an 8087 coprocessor. Chapter 4 requires knowledge of electronic circuit construction, breadboarding, wirewrapping, and familiarity with terms such as inverters and op amps.

This is an unusual book, in the expanding new field of artificial neural networks, in that it is an introduction to computer modelling and hardware experiments. I hope the book will open up new avenues of experimentation for computer hackers and researchers in artificial intelligence.

1
Parallel Distributed Processing

In this chapter I will discuss the limitations to present day von Neumann computers and the limitations to computing. After a discussion of parallel architecture and special purpose computers I will discuss the transputer and the connection machine. This will lead into a discussion of neural network architectures for computing.

LIMITS TO COMPUTATION

It is reasonable to expect that there are limits to computation. The first limit I will discuss is heat dissipation in logic. The thermodynamical minimum of energy per logical act as given by von Neumann (1966), is

$$kT \log_e 2 = 3 \times 10^{-14} \text{ erg.}$$

where k is the Boltzmann constant and T is temperature in Kelvin. The human brain dissipates 25×10^{-10} watts per neuron or 3×10^{-3} erg per binary act. Information processing in a general purpose computer is an irreversible act. For example, in the equation

$$3 + 2 = 5$$

there is more information on the left hand side than on the right hand side. The answer, 5, can be produced in many ways. So the act of information processing is irreversible.

The logical AND function is a perfect example of information loss in a computer. Figure 1-1 is a truth table for the AND function.

Fig. 1-1. AND function truth table.

INPUTS		OUT
0	0	0
0	1	0
1	0	0
1	1	1

It is clearly seen from this truth table that 1 is produced in only one way, whereas 0 is produced in three ways. Digital computers contain information by virtue of being in a state of nonequilibrium. In otherwords, a dissipative state.

The minimum energy dissipation is of the order of kT. In a digital computer the electrical signals change the voltage potential in other spatial regions of the system. Electrons are dispersed by an order of kT by thermal agitation or thermal noise. This is the equivalent of **kT/q** in volts if **q** is the charge on the electron. At room temperature kT/q = 0.025 volts. Logical computations must be greater than 0.025 volts because logical processes are nonlinear. Neuron voltages are a few kT/q volts. At a lower temperature smaller kT/q values can be used for logical processing. The point is this: the higher kT/q required for logic operations the higher the power dissipation.

These high power dissipation calculations have assumed that information processing is a non-reversible process. Fredkin and Toffali (1982) have designed a reversible logic element. In this logical processing element, no information is lost, like that in the AND gate. The NOT gate is an example of a reversible logic element where no information is lost. One of the logic gates suggested by Fredkin and Toffali is the *controlled* NOT gate, which is shown in Fig. 1-2.

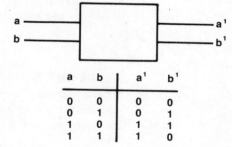

Fig. 1-2. CONTROLLED NOT gate truth table.

a	b	a^1	b^1
0	0	0	0
0	1	0	1
1	0	1	1
1	1	1	0

They also discuss the *controlled controlled* NOT gate shown in Fig. 1-3.

Bennett (1979) has shown that a reversible computer can be built with Fredkin logic. The energy dissipated in a reversible computer is virtually zero. Using the *controlled* NOT gate and the *controlled controlled* NOT gate, Feynman (1985) has constructed hypothetical adders and other arithmetic logic units. Furthermore, with no heat dissipation in these units, he has shown that there is no theoretical reason to not be able to assemble computers using

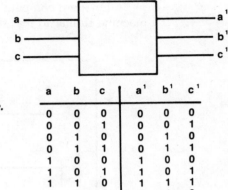

Fig. 1-3. CONTROLLED CON-
TROLLED NOT gate truth table.

a	b	c	a¹	b¹	c¹
0	0	0	0	0	0
0	0	1	0	0	1
0	1	0	0	1	0
0	1	1	0	1	1
1	0	0	1	0	0
1	0	1	1	0	1
1	1	0	1	1	1
1	1	1	1	1	0

quantum or atomic size logic elements. So there is no physical limit to the smallness of a computer. In Chapter 5, I will discuss the work of Forrest Carter on molecular electronic devices.

PARALLEL PROCESSING ARCHITECTURE

Almost all computers today are von Neumann architecture, this means they process information serially. As a result of this serial processing there is a bottleneck. The "von Neumann bottleneck" hinders the flow of signals between the central processing unit (CPU) and the memory, limiting the speed of the entire system. A schematic of this bottleneck is shown in Fig. 1-4.

The CPU is surrounded by the input, output, and memory unit for storage of intermediate results. The stored results are retrieved as needed and the final result is sent to the output unit. The bottleneck is clearly illustrated in a simple program such as:

$$x = 5$$
$$y = z + x$$

Most of the program is involved with where to put or get something rather than the actual computation.

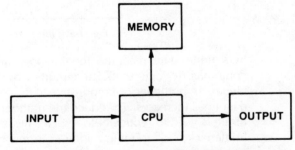

Fig. 1-4. Schematic of von Neumann bottleneck.

All modern computers are derived from a so-called classical finite state machine similar to that shown in Fig. 1-5.

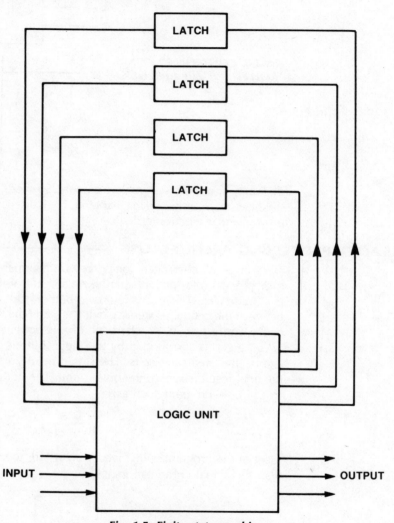

Fig. 1-5. Finite state machine.

In a finite state machine the memory unit is latches and the CPU is a combinatoric logic unit. The circuit is completely parallel and has no von Neumann bottleneck. If more state variables are needed then the number of data lines increases. To reduce the number of lines a binary encoding technique is used to reduce N to $\log_2 N$. This is the source of the von Neumann bottleneck. This modified finite state machine is shown in Fig. 1-6.

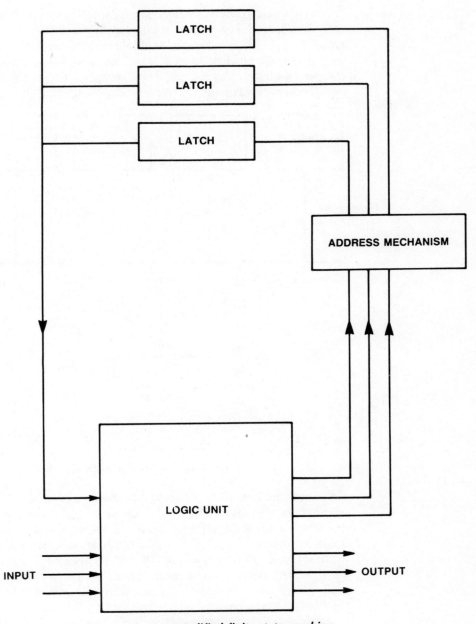

Fig. 1-6. Modified finite state machine.

An obvious solution is to build an all parallel machine. There are a number of architectures for computer systems. They can be grouped into two main types: SIMD, or single instruction multiple data streams, and MIMD, or multiple instruction multiple data streams. These two types of systems are broken down into several topologies for the actual computer construction.

The simplest parallel machine is shown in Fig. 1-7.

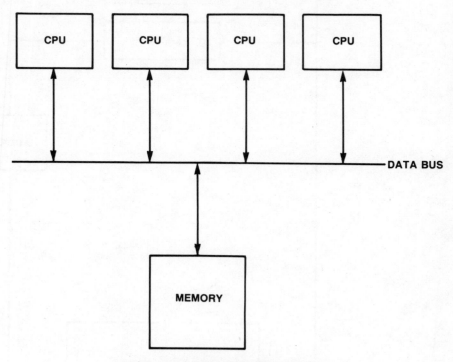

Fig. 1-7. Simplified parallel machine.

In this configuration there are several processors, all of which share the same memory. The operating system must avoid using the same memory cells for more than one processor. Furthermore, the operating system must synchronize use of the memory bus. This memory bus leads to a bottleneck and suggests the next type architecture. Figure 1-8 shows a multibus system. In this system the operating system would control data flow between the processors and the memory unit. The chief difficulty with this system is the complexity of the operating system.

The switching architecture avoids bottlenecks at data busses and makes for a simple operating system. Figure 1-9 shows a bottleneck-free architecture. This system uses a network of programmable switches similar to a telephone switching network. This type of parallel computer can be very efficient because each processor is in essence hardwired to its memory unit. The primary diffi-

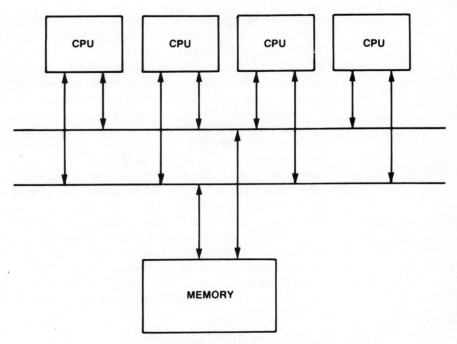

Fig. 1-8. Multibus parallel machine.

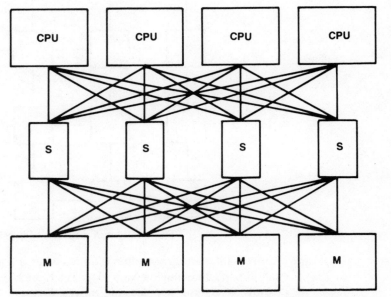

Fig. 1-9. Switchable network of processors. M-memory, S-switch.

culty again is in programming. The operating system must control the switching network. This switching network can be done away with in other types of parallel architectures.

The hypercube architecture is one type of system that does not use a switching network. The system can have, for example, 64 processors, each with its own memory. Each processor/memory occupies a corner of a hypercube. The number of corners of the hypercube is given by 2^N, where **N** is the number of dimensions. For our example, **N** = 6 because 2^6 = 64. In our example each processor/memory node occupies a corner of a six-dimensional hypercube and each node is connected to its six nearest neighbors. Hypercubes are very efficient for certain algorithms. For example, often each processor would be asked to model a small section of a system. Each processor could represent a single galaxy and the entire hypercube of processors a galactic cluster for modelling the evolution of the cluster.

For other algorithms the hypercube is not as efficient, and special purpose parallel processing machines may be needed. Special purpose computers are problem oriented. For a given problem, a computer is designed and built to solve it. Figure 1-10 shows a mesh configuration. This configuration is excellent for pattern recognition. Each node processes data signals from one pixel or picture element.

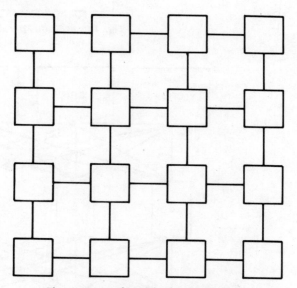

Fig. 1-10. Mesh network of processors.

Artificial intelligence often requires what is known as a tree search. For example, in game playing each move is a branch of the tree and each branch or move leads to other possible moves. Figure 1-11 shows a tree used for searching. These searches can be very slow with a von Neumann computer,

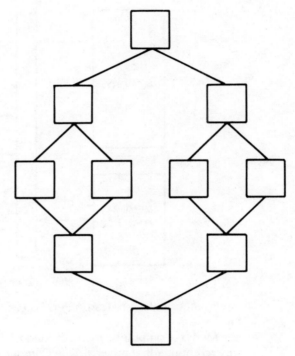

Fig. 1-11. Tree search processor.

but with a parallel machine it can be very fast. Each node in the tree is a processor.

There are even more special purpose parallel computers in operation. At Fermi National Laboratory, Thomas Nash and his collaborators built a special purpose computer for high energy physics data collection and analysis. Another special purpose computer, for Monte Carlo simulation in statistical physics, has been built by Condon and Ogielski of AT&T Bell Laboratories. Also built at AT&T Bell Labs is a special purpose computer for playing chess. This computer has been discussed by Bernstein (1984).

There are two exciting recent developments I'd like to mention. One is the Transputer and the second is the Connection Machine.

The *Transputer* from Inmos is one of the most exciting computer developments in years. A diagram of the Transputer is shown in Fig. 1-12. The Transputer contains 2K of memory, a 32-bit processor, a memory interface, and four interface links. The Transputer is in essence a building block for parallel processing. Transputers can easily be assembled in many of the topologies discussed so far. Each Transputer link contains input and output lines. In assembling a parallel system the output lines of a Transputer building block are connected to the input lines of another. There are a total of four such

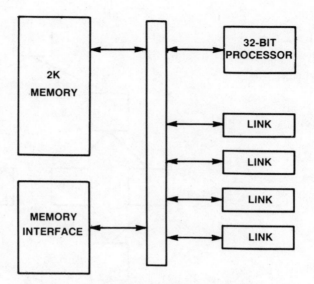

Fig. 1-12. Schematic of transputer chip.

input/output links per Transputer. So each Transputer can be connected to four others.

Meiko Computers Inc., Oakland, California, is selling a personal supercomputer that they call *The Computing Surface*. It contains 150, 32-bit Transputers and provides 1000 million instructions per second (1 GIP). The entire system can fit into a standard 19-inch rack mount. Configuring the topology of the processors is performed manually using jumper leads on the back plane. A newer model is planned for software configuration.

Another exciting recent development in computing is the *connectionist architecture*. Connection machines are massively parallel networks of simple processors. Heretofore I have discussed course grained architecture i.e., computers with several hundreds of processing elements. Connectionist architectures are fine grained with tens of thousands to millions of processors. The human brain provides an existence proof that massive parallel processing with billions of processing elements is possible. Often in connectionist architecture the individual processors do not have much memory associated with them. Long-term storage is accomplished by the interconnection of the processors themselves. In Chapter 4, I will discuss how to build a small eight processor artificial neural network, or connection machine. The processing units in most connection machines do not follow complex instructions or programs. Each processor is capable of only very simple actions such as threshold logic. The entire connection machine is usually controlled by a host computer.

The rest of this book is about a specialized type of connection machine often called an artificial neural network. Each processor is a simple threshold logic unit. The stored data is stored in the interconnection network of the processors. The entire system is interfaced to a host computer.

Before I move into a discussion of the theory of parallel distributed processing with threshold logic units, I should mention Thinking Machines Corporation's Connection Machine, developed by Hills et. al. (1985). This machine is called a *connection machine* but there are significant differences between it and artificial neural networks. The Connection Machine of Hills uses 64K processors. Each processor is associated with a small cell of 4K of memory. Hills' machine is much more general purpose than the connection architecture I will discuss. The artificial neural networks of only tens to thousands processors are best used as special purpose coprocessors for pattern recognition, linear optimization, robotics, etc. No one has yet built a million or a billion logic unit artificial neural network. Who knows what that might be capable of? As we know, a wet computer based on 100 billion logic units or neurons is self-conscious.

2

Mathematics and Theory of Parallel Distributed Processing

This chapter introduces the mathematical methods and fundamental theoretical concepts of parallel distributed processing using threshold logic devices. The basic concepts of model neural networks can be described by vector analysis and linear algebra.

VECTOR ALGEBRA

A vector can be represented on an X-Y coordinate system as shown in Fig. 2-1. The vector of Fig. 2-1 has components $x = 3$ and $Y = 4$, which can be represented by $v = (3\ 4)$. In this book lower case letters represent vectors, uppercase will represent matrices. Other variables will be obvious from context.

A three dimensional vector would have three components, $v = (x\ Y\ z)$ and an n-dimensional vector would have n components, $v = (v_1\ v_2\ v_3 \bullet \bullet \bullet v_n)$. Where the v_i's represent the components for the dimension i up to n dimensions. The vector $v = (3\ 4)$, can be multiplied by a number, A, as follows

$$A \bullet v = (A \bullet 3\ A \bullet 4).$$

And for an n-dimensional vector you get

$$A \bullet v = (A \bullet v_1\ A \bullet v_2\ A \bullet v_3 \bullet \bullet \bullet A \bullet v_n).$$

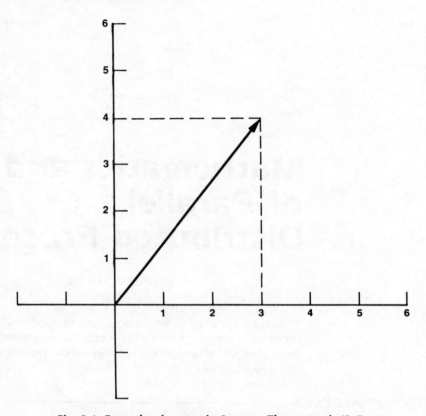

Fig. 2-1. Example of vector in 2-space. The vector is (3,4).

Vector addition is done by adding the components. For example, given two vectors, a = (12 4) and b = (−6 1), then their sum is

$$a + b = (12 - 6 \quad 4 + 1) = (6 \quad 5)$$

Multiplication of two vectors is a little less obvious. Vectors can be multiplied in two ways. One is called the dot product a • b, the other is called the cross product a × b. The dot product is also called the scalar product or the inner product.

The inner product is given by the relation

$$a \cdot b = (a_1b_1 \quad a_2b_2 \quad a_3b_3 \cdot \cdot \cdot).$$

The magnitude of vector a is represented by |a| and similarly for vector b. The magnitude of a vector is found by taking the square root of the sum of the square of the components of the vector. For example, in n dimensions you have

$$|a| = (a_1^2 + a_2^2 + \cdots + a_n^2)^{1/2}$$

$$|a| = (\sum_i a_i^2)^{1/2}.$$

The angle between the two vectors can be found by the relation:

$$\cos \theta = \frac{a \cdot b}{|a|\, |b|}$$

This equation can be written in terms of the components as:

$$\cos \theta = \frac{\sum_i v_i w_i}{(\sum_i v_i^2)^{1/2}\, (\sum_i w_i^2)^{1/2}}$$

An example of the use of this relation in parallel distributed processing is shown in Fig. 2-2. Given a processor, u, it receives its input form n process v_i. This output process u is given by the inner product of the input process v_i and the strength of the weight of each process w_i.

$$u = w \cdot v$$

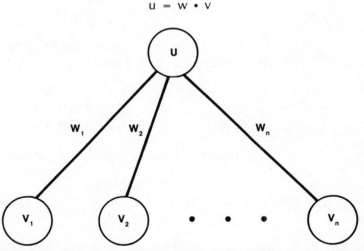

Fig. 2-2. Inner product of input vector, v, and strength vector w, results in scalar u.

In the dot product the commutative law holds:

$$w \cdot v = v \cdot w$$

The cross product, also called the outer product, results in a vector. The vector product in three dimensional space can be represented by

$$a \times b = [(a_2b_3 - a_3b_2) \, (a_3b_1 - a_1b_3) \, (a_1b_2 - a_2b_1)]$$

MATRICES

A matrix is an array of elements or real numbers. For example:

$$M = \begin{bmatrix} 3 & 2 & 9 \\ 7 & 6 & 0 \\ 1 & 4 & 2 \end{bmatrix}$$

M is a three dimensional matrix, or a 3×3 matrix. Matrices need not be square. For example:

$$P = \begin{bmatrix} 2 & 0 \\ 7 & 1 \\ 5 & 4 \end{bmatrix} \qquad N = \begin{bmatrix} 1 \\ 0 \\ 1 \end{bmatrix}$$

P is a 3×2 matrix and N is a 3×1 matrix.

It is sometimes convenient to think of a vector as a one dimensional matrix.

$$V = [3 \ 1 \ 0]$$

Multiplication of a matrix by a scalar is the same as multiplication of a vector by a scalar. Each element in the matrix is multiplied by the scalar.

$$3P = \begin{bmatrix} 3 \cdot 2 & 3 \cdot 0 \\ 3 \cdot 7 & 3 \cdot 1 \\ 3 \cdot 5 & 3 \cdot 4 \end{bmatrix} = \begin{bmatrix} 6 & 0 \\ 21 & 3 \\ 15 & 12 \end{bmatrix}$$

Addition of matrices is similar to addition of vectors. For example:

$$M_1 = \begin{bmatrix} 1 & 0 & 5 \\ 0 & 7 & 2 \\ 4 & 6 & 6 \end{bmatrix} \qquad M_2 = \begin{bmatrix} 6 & 9 & -3 \\ 5 & 2 & 0 \\ -8 & 4 & 4 \end{bmatrix}$$

then

$$M_1 + M_2 = \begin{bmatrix} 1+6 & 0+9 & 5-3 \\ 0+5 & 7+2 & 2+0 \\ 4-8 & 3+4 & 6+4 \end{bmatrix} = \begin{bmatrix} 7 & 9 & 2 \\ 5 & 9 & 2 \\ -4 & 7 & 10 \end{bmatrix}$$

This has application in memory storage. If each matrix represents one memory then the sum of the two matrices results in a storage matrix for the two memory states.

A very important concept is the multiplication of a vector by a matrix. This can be used in pattern recognition and memory recall. For example given a vector:

$$v = \begin{bmatrix} 2 \\ 9 \\ 7 \end{bmatrix}$$

and a matrix:

$$M = \begin{bmatrix} 1 & 0 & 5 \\ 0 & 7 & 2 \\ 4 & 3 & 6 \end{bmatrix}$$

the inner product is found as follows:

$$u = M v = \begin{bmatrix} 1 & 0 & 5 \\ 0 & 7 & 2 \\ 4 & 3 & 6 \end{bmatrix} \begin{bmatrix} 2 \\ 9 \\ 7 \end{bmatrix}$$

$$u = \begin{bmatrix} 1 \cdot 2 + 0 \cdot 9 + 5 \cdot 7 \\ 0 \cdot 2 + 7 \cdot 9 + 2 \cdot 7 \\ 4 \cdot 2 + 3 \cdot 9 + 6 \cdot 7 \end{bmatrix} = \begin{matrix} 37 \\ 77 \\ 77 \end{matrix}$$

Notice that the inner product of a matrix with a vector is a vector. The matrix need not be square. As shown in the following example:

$$K = \begin{bmatrix} 3 & 7 & 1 \\ 0 & 1 & 2 \end{bmatrix} \qquad t = \begin{bmatrix} 1 \\ 0 \\ 3 \end{bmatrix}$$

$$q = K t = \begin{bmatrix} 3 & 7 & 1 \\ 0 & 1 & 2 \end{bmatrix} \begin{bmatrix} 1 \\ 0 \\ 3 \end{bmatrix} = \begin{bmatrix} 3 \cdot 1 + 7 \cdot 0 + 1 \cdot 3 \\ 0 \cdot 1 + 1 \cdot 0 + 2 \cdot 3 \end{bmatrix} = \begin{bmatrix} 6 \\ 6 \end{bmatrix} = 6 \begin{bmatrix} 1 \\ 1 \end{bmatrix}$$

This is sufficiently important to be written in symbolic terms.

$$u = M v$$

$$(i^{th} \text{ component of } u) = (i^{th} \text{ row of } M)(v)$$

A convenient way of thinking of this operation is as a mapping, where v is mapped to u by the operation M (see Fig. 2-3).

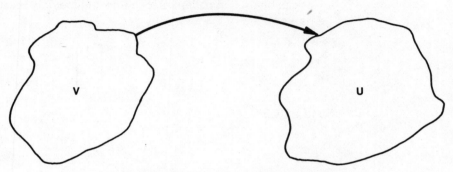

Fig. 2-3. Map of v to u, by process, M.

This mapping of one state into another is analogous to a one-layer parallel distributed processing system. Figure 2-4 shows *n* input units and *p* output units. Each input processor is connected to each output processor by a connection strength, M_{pn}. Where M_{pn} represents the pn^{th} element in the matrix M. Each output unit computes the inner product of its weight vector and the input vector. In other words the output at the ith output processor is found by computing the inner product of the input vector with the weight for the ith processor.

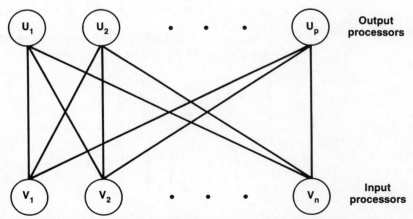

Fig. 2-4. Two layer process. All processors at v, are connected to all processors at u.

The component of the input vector is the values of the input units. The weight vector for the ith process is the ith row of the strength matrix M.

The technique can be extended to multilayered systems where the output of one layer becomes the input of the next layer. In Fig. 2-5, the processors at a, are connected to each of the processors at b. These are in turn connected to each of the c processors. An input vector at a is mapped to b by the connection strength matrix Y. Vector b is then mapped to vector c by connection strength Z. This can be represented symbolically as

$$c = Z(Ya).$$

In other words the matrix vector product of Ya results in the vector b and the matrix vector product Zb results in c.

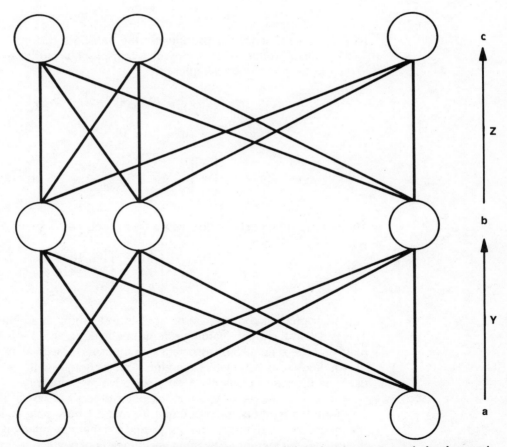

Fig. 2-5. Three layer process. Processors at a are connected to processors at b, by the matrix, Y. Processors at b are connected to those at c, by matrix Z.

A very important mathematical technique in parallel distributed processing theory is the transpose and outer product of a vector. The *transpose* of a $n \times m$ *matrix* is a $m \times n$ *matrix*. If the matrix is a one dimensional matrix, i.e. a vector, then the transpose is found as demonstrated in the following example. Given a vector

$$v = [3 \quad 7 \quad 9 \quad 2]$$

then the transpose of v is given by

$$v^t = \begin{bmatrix} 3 \\ 7 \\ 9 \\ 2 \end{bmatrix}$$

Notice the superscript *t*. This indicates the transpose operation.

The inner product of a vector with a transposed vector gives a scalar, as shown in the following example:

$$v = [9 \quad 7 \quad 3]$$

$$u = [5 \quad 2 \quad 0]$$

$$vu^t = [9 \quad 7 \quad 3] \begin{bmatrix} 5 \\ 2 \\ 0 \end{bmatrix} = 9 \cdot 5 + 7 \cdot 2 + 3 \cdot 0 = 59$$

The outer product of a vector with a transposed vector gives a matrix.

$$uv^t = [5 \quad 2 \quad 0] \begin{bmatrix} 9 \\ 7 \\ 3 \end{bmatrix} = \begin{bmatrix} 45 & 18 & 0 \\ 35 & 14 & 0 \\ 15 & 6 & 0 \end{bmatrix}$$

The outer product concept can be applied to learning in a neural network. This is called the Hebb learning rule (Rumelhart, et. al. 1986). A particular matrix can be generated by associating an input vector with an output vector. This is known as associative learning. The technique will be used in an example program in Chapter 3 on associative memories.

For any given vector v, when the outer product of v with its transpose v^t is found, a memory matrix unique for that memory state is generated. If the inner product of this memory state and the memory matrix is found then the result is the memory. The input vector need not be the pure memory state but only a partial memory. When this partial memory state is operated on by the memory matrix the inner product will give the complete and correct memory state. Chapter 3 contains a program to demonstrate this and Chapter 4 describes a circuit to implement this with electronic components.

What is not obvious from the above is that a given memory matrix can store more than one memory state. The actual number of memories depends on the size of the matrix.

Threshold Logic and Nonlinear Systems

The Human brain is a massive parallel personal computer based on organic threshold logic devices. These logic devices are known as neurons. A neuron is sketched in Fig. 2-6 and shown in Photo 2-1.

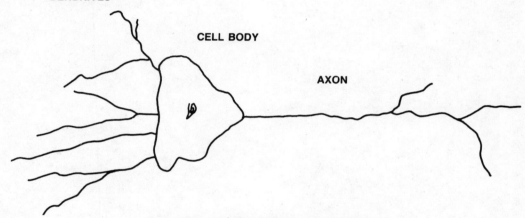

DENDRITES

CELL BODY

AXON

Fig. 2-6. Simplified diagram of a neuron.

The cell body has one or more output lines called the axon. The input lines are called dendrites. There are about 1000 dendrite connections to an average neuron in the human brain. The neurons are interconnected by a synapse. A neuron can have both excitatory and inhibitory connections. An excitatory connection tells the neuron to fire and an inhibitory connection tells a neuron to not fire. The input signals are summed in the neuron. At a certain threshold level the neuron will fire and below this level not fire. This is diagrammed in Fig. 2-7. If the sum of the input signal I_{in} is less than threshold, I_t, then v_{out} goes low, logic 0. If the sum of input signal I_{in} is above threshold I_t, then v_{out} goes high, logic 1. This idea can be represented algebraically as follows.

$$v_{out} = \begin{cases} 1 & > I_t \\ & \text{if } I_{in} \\ 0 & < I_t \end{cases}$$

Photo 2-1. Neural circuit cultured on a 68000 microprocessor. (Courtesy of John Stevens and Judy Trogadis, Playfair Memorial Neuroscience Unit, University of Toronto.)

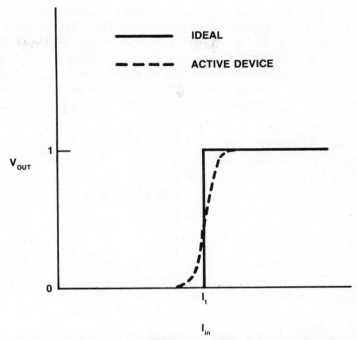

Fig. 2-7. Threshold logic device transfer curve. Solid curve is ideal device and dotted curve is active, real device.

Software implementation of this idea is presented in Chapter 3.

This model is a little naive, since the synapse connections to the inputs of the threshold logic device have not been considered. In hardware implementation of threshold logic circuits the synapse is a resistive interconnection between logic devices. A less naive model in algebraic terms is given below.

$$V_{out} = \begin{cases} 1 & \text{if} \sum_{j \neq i} W_{ij}v_j & > I_t \\ 0 & & < I_t \end{cases}$$

In this relation the v_j is the input signal to neuron j and W_{ij} is the conductance of the connection between the ith and the jth neuron. Each threshold logic unit randomly and asynchronously computes whether it is above or below threshold and readjusts accordingly. Therefore a network of these threshold logic units is a parallel computer.

This parallel computer can be used in optimization problems, and content-addressable memories. The content-addressable memory implementation of these parallel computation circuits will be discussed at length in this book.

The information storage algorithm for content-addressable memories, discussed in this book, is called the Hebb learning rule. A memory state is given as a binary vector. In a binary vector all the elements are either 1 or 0. The outer product of this memory vector with its transpose gives a storage matrix. Taking an example. The ASCII code for the letter A is given by the standard binary representation (0 1 0 0 0 0 0 1). The outer product of this eight-dimensional binary vector with its transpose is given in the algorithm.

$$\begin{bmatrix} 0 \\ 1 \\ 0 \\ 0 \\ 0 \\ 0 \\ 0 \\ 1 \end{bmatrix} [0\ 1\ 0\ 0\ 0\ 0\ 0\ 1] = \begin{bmatrix} 0 & 0 & 0 & 0 & 0 & 0 & 0 & 0 \\ 0 & 1 & 0 & 0 & 0 & 0 & 0 & 1 \\ 0 & 0 & 0 & 0 & 0 & 0 & 0 & 0 \\ 0 & 0 & 0 & 0 & 0 & 0 & 0 & 0 \\ 0 & 0 & 0 & 0 & 0 & 0 & 0 & 0 \\ 0 & 0 & 0 & 0 & 0 & 0 & 0 & 0 \\ 0 & 0 & 0 & 0 & 0 & 0 & 0 & 0 \\ 0 & 1 & 0 & 0 & 0 & 0 & 0 & 1 \end{bmatrix}$$

This storage algorithm can be represented in algebraic terms as

$$W = m^t\, m$$

W is the information storage matrix, m is the memory vector and m^t is the transpose of vector m.

This model does not consider an important point. It doesn't make much sense to have a neuron connected to itself, therefore the elements W_{ii} should be set to zero. Hopfield (1982, 1984) and McEliece, et. al. (1985), have shown that if W_{ii} is not zero then the hardware implementation of the model can result in chaotic oscillations. The correct algebraic relation is

$$W = m^t\, m - I_n$$

Where I_n is the n × n identity matrix. So the storage algorithm consists of the outer product of the memory vector with itself, except that 0's are placed on the diagonal. Next is an example using the ASCII code for the letter Z.

$$\begin{bmatrix} 0 \\ 1 \\ 0 \\ 1 \\ 1 \\ 0 \\ 1 \\ 0 \end{bmatrix} [0\ 1\ 0\ 1\ 1\ 0\ 1\ 0] = \begin{bmatrix} 0 & 0 & 0 & 0 & 0 & 0 & 0 & 0 \\ 0 & 0 & 0 & 1 & 1 & 0 & 1 & 0 \\ 0 & 0 & 0 & 0 & 0 & 0 & 0 & 0 \\ 0 & 1 & 0 & 0 & 1 & 0 & 1 & 0 \\ 0 & 1 & 0 & 1 & 0 & 0 & 1 & 0 \\ 0 & 0 & 0 & 0 & 0 & 0 & 0 & 0 \\ 0 & 1 & 0 & 1 & 1 & 0 & 0 & 0 \\ 0 & 0 & 0 & 0 & 0 & 0 & 0 & 0 \end{bmatrix}$$

Hopfield (1982, 1984) has shown that the storage matrix must be symmetric, $W_{ij} = W_{ji}$, that $W_{ii} = 0$ and the matrix must be dilute. That is, there must be a smaller number of 1's than 0's in the matrix. If the matrix is not symmetric, $W_{ij} \neq W_{ji}$, then nonstable states and false memory states will be produced.

To show how this storage matrix can produce the correct memory state, an eight-dimensional binary vector with bit errors when multiplied by this storage matrix to give the inner product will generate the correct memory state. The number of bit errors can not be too great, but a partial memory will certainly work to give the complete memory state. For example:

$$
\begin{bmatrix}
0 & 0 & 0 & 0 & 0 & 0 & 0 & 0 \\
0 & 0 & 0 & 1 & 1 & 0 & 1 & 0 \\
0 & 0 & 0 & 0 & 0 & 0 & 0 & 0 \\
0 & 1 & 0 & 0 & 1 & 0 & 1 & 0 \\
0 & 1 & 0 & 1 & 0 & 0 & 1 & 0 \\
0 & 0 & 0 & 0 & 0 & 0 & 0 & 0 \\
0 & 1 & 0 & 1 & 1 & 0 & 0 & 0 \\
0 & 0 & 0 & 0 & 0 & 0 & 0 & 0
\end{bmatrix}
\begin{bmatrix}
0 \\ 1 \\ 0 \\ 0 \\ 1 \\ 0 \\ 0 \\ 1
\end{bmatrix}
=
\begin{bmatrix}
0 \\ 1 \\ 0 \\ 1 \\ 1 \\ 0 \\ 1 \\ 0
\end{bmatrix}
$$

The number of bit errors is called Hamming distance. Given the two vectors

$$v = 0 \; 1 \; 0 \; 0 \; 1 \; 0 \; 0 \; 1$$

$$u = 0 \; 1 \; 0 \; 1 \; 1 \; 0 \; 1 \; 1$$

the Hamming distance in this example is 3. Only vectors of equal dimensionality can be compared.

Hopfield (1982, 1984) has shown that if the matrix is symmetric and dilute with $W_{ii} = 0$, and if we define the dimension of the matrix as n then m memories can be stored. Where m = 0.15n. This relation was found by computer experiments similar to these in Chapter 3. Table 2-1 is a list of the number of memories for a given matrix size. Notice in the table the actual number of memories has been rounded down to the nearest whole number. It doesn't make sense to store a fraction of a memory state.

Table 2-1

Memories	Neurons (matrix size)
1	8
2	16
3	24
4	32
5	40

All of this can be expressed more formally to assist in writing code for a digital computer simulation.

The Hebb rule is used to determine the values of the W matrix. This is a vector outer product rule.

$$W_{ij} = \begin{cases} 1 \text{ if } \sum_{i=1}^{R} v_i^s u_j^s > 0 \\ 0 \quad \text{otherwise} \end{cases}$$

This states that the element W_{ij} is found by summing the outer product of the input vector element j and output vector element i. It is a simple outer product of these vectors. The W_{ij} element is then found by summing the W_i matrices. In other words the outer product of the input vector u^s and the output vector v^s results in a matrix W^s. The elements of the final W matrix are found by summing the W^s matrices.

$$W = \sum_{s=1}^{\text{all states}} W^s$$

The sum is over all memory states. Each memory produces one matrix. The total memory matrix is the sum of these matrices. Hopfield (1982, 1984), has shown that if

$$W_{ii} = 0 \text{ and } W_{ij} = W_{ji}$$

then stable states will exist and the network will not oscillate chaotically.

Given the W matrix, then the matrix vector product, the inner product, of this W with u^s, the input vector state, will result in the output vector v^s

$$v^s = Wu^s$$

The elements of this vector v^s are given by:

$$v_i^s = \sum_{j=1}^{N} W_{ij} u_j^s \quad \text{(state s)}$$

What this says is that, output vector element v_i is given by the sum of the products of elements $W_{ij} u_j$ summed over all j. For example:

$$W = \begin{bmatrix} W_{11} & W_{12} & W_{13} \\ W_{21} & W_{22} & W_{23} \\ W_{31} & W_{32} & W_{33} \end{bmatrix}$$

$$u_s = [u_1^s \ u_2^s \ u_3^s]$$

then

$$v^s = \begin{bmatrix} W_{11} & W_{12} & W_{13} \\ W_{21} & W_{22} & W_{23} \\ W_{31} & W_{32} & W_{33} \end{bmatrix} \begin{bmatrix} u_1^s \\ u_2^s \\ u_3^s \end{bmatrix} = \begin{bmatrix} v_1^s \\ v_2^s \\ v_3^s \end{bmatrix}$$

$$v_1^s = W_{11}u_1^s + W_{12}u_2^s + W_{13}u_3^s$$

$$v_2^s = W_{21}u_1^s + W_{22}u_2^s + W_{23}u_3^s$$

$$v_3^s = W_{31}u_1^s + W_{32}u_2^s + W_{33}u_3^s.$$

This output vector should include a term for the information input, bias and noise. If these terms are added together to give one term I_i, then you get:

$$v_i = \sum_j W_{ij}u_j + I_i.$$

The actual vector is given by:

$$v_i = \begin{cases} 1 & \text{if } \sum_j W_{ij}u_j + I_i > I_t \\ \\ 0 & \text{otherwise} \end{cases}$$

Where I_t is threshold (see Fig. 2-7) and W_{ij} is the conductance of the connection between threshold logic units i and j. In otherwords W_{ij} is the synaptic strength.

The energy corresponding to the stable states as given by Hopfield (1982, 1984) is:

$$E = - \frac{1}{2} \sum_{i=1}^{N} \sum_{j=1}^{N} W_{ij}v_iv_j$$

Where $W_{ij} = W_{ji}$ and $W_{ii} = 0$.

Goles and Vichniac (1986) write this equation in a form that clearly shows how to calculate the energy function.

$$E = - \frac{1}{2} \sum_{i=1}^{N} v_i^{t+1} \sum_{j=1}^{N} W_{ij}v_j^t$$

This energy calculation will be discussed at length in Chapter 3 with a digital computer simulation.

3

Digital Computer Simulations

In this chapter elementary digital computer simulations of neural networks will be discussed. The equations from Chapter 2 will be used to develop computer algorithms.

CONTENT-ADDRESSABLE MEMORIES AND ENERGY CALCULATIONS ─────────

When the inner product between a vector and a matrix is found, a vector is generated. The concepts discussed in Chapter 2 will be reiterated here. If the starting vector doesn't differ too much from the stored memory state in the matrix then the resulting vector is the correct memory state. This has obvious applications as a content-addressable memory.

Some examples will make this more clear. Figure 3-1A shows a partial memory state for the complete memory state of Fig. 3-1B. If the partial memory state is digitized and operated on by an appropriate memory matrix then the correct memory is generated or recalled.

Figure 3-2A shows a partial spectral pattern. In this partial memory state no fine structure is observed. But when this spectrum is digitized and operated on by the appropriate storage matrix then the spectrum of Fig. 3-2B is recalled or generated.

This memory recall often happens to people, also. You see a person in the distance with lime-green socks but other details are not clear. Then you recall your friend had lime-green socks. This produces in your mind, the entire picture of your friend. Further examples of content-addressable memory are easy to conceive. Looking in a tool box you might see only five percent of a wrench handle because the rest of the wrench is hidden by other tools. But this is enough of a pattern for you to recognize it as the wrench you need.

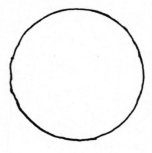

Fig. 3-1A. Partial memory state.   *Fig. 3-1B. Complete memory state.*

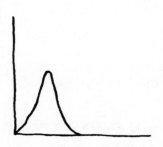

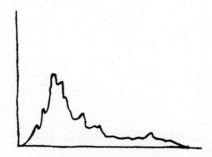

Fig. 3-2A. Partial spectral pattern.   *Fig. 3-2B. Complete spectral pattern.*

The first step in an algorithm for content-addressing is to find the inner product of a vector and a matrix.

$$V^s = Tu^s$$

The connection strength matrix T, is given by:

$$T = \begin{bmatrix} T_{11} & T_{12} & \cdots & T_{1N} \\ T_{21} & T_{22} & \cdots & T_{2N} \\ \vdots & & & \\ T_{i1} & T_{i2} & \cdots & T_{NN} \end{bmatrix}$$

It was shown that the elements of the resulting vector from the inner product of T with vector u, is:

$$V_i^s = \sum_{j=1}^{N} T_{ij} u_j^s.$$

It was further shown that the diagonal elements of the T matrix must be zero and the matrix should be symmetric and dilute. Symmetric means:

$$T_{ij} = T_{ji}$$

A dilute matrix means that the matrix contains more 0's than 1's.

NEURON4P

```
10 CLS
20 INPUT "INPUT RANDOM SEED ";SEED
30 RANDOMIZE SEED
40 INPUT "ENTER THE NUMBER OF NEURONS (100 MAXIMUM) ";N
50 INPUT "INPUT THE THRESHOLD VALUE (0 TO 2 ARE REASONABLE
VALUES) ";IO
60 INPUT "ENTER THE VALUE OF THE INFORMATION (0 TO 1 IS A GOOD
VALUE) ";INFO
70 INPUT "DO YOU WANT TO ENTER THE INPUT VECTOR YOURSELF
(1/YES, 0/NO)? ";VECTOR
80 INPUT "DO YOU WANT TO INPUT THE T MATRIX (1/Y 0/NO)
";MATRIX
90 DIM T(100,100),V(100),U(100)
100 REM FILL T(I,J) MATRIX
110 IF MATRIX-0 THEN 190
120 FOR I-1 TO N
130 FOR J-1 TO N
140 PRINT "T(";I;",";J;") "
150 INPUT T(I,J)
160 NEXT J
170 NEXT I
180 GOTO 360 : 'FILL INPUT VECTOR
190 FOR I-1 TO N
200 FOR J-1 TO N
210 R-RND(1)
220 IF R<.75 THEN R-0 ELSE R-+1 : REM DILUTE MATRIX
230 T(I,J)-R
240 NEXT J
250 LPRINT
260 NEXT I
270 FOR I-1 TO N
280 FOR J-1 TO N
290 IF I-J THEN T(I,J)-0
```

```
300 T(J,I)=T(I,J)
310 LPRINT T(I,J);
320 NEXT J
330 LPRINT
340 NEXT I
350 LPRINT : LPRINT : LPRINT
360 REM FILL INPUT VECTOR U
370 IF VECTOR=0 THEN 430
380 FOR I=1 TO N
390 PRINT "INPUT U(";I;")"
400 INPUT U(I)
410 NEXT I
420 GOTO 470 : 'BEGIN CALCULATIONS OF OUTPUT VECTOR
430 FOR I=1 TO N
440 GOSUB 670
450 U(I)=R
460 NEXT I
470 REM BEGIN CALCULATION
480 FOR I=1 TO N
490 FOR J=1 TO N
500 SIGMA=T(I,J)*U(J)+SIGMA
510 NEXT J
520 SIGMA=SIGMA+INFO
530 IF SIGMA > IO THEN SIGMA=1 ELSE SIGMA=0
540 U(I)=SIGMA
550 SIGMA=0
560 NEXT I
570 FOR I=1 TO N
580 LPRINT U(I);
590 NEXT I
600 LPRINT : LPRINT
610 FOR I=1 TO N
620 LPRINT U(I);
630 NEXT I
640 LPRINT : LPRINT
650 LPRINT : LPRINT
660 GOTO 360
670 R=RND(1)
680 IF R< .5 THEN R=0 ELSE R=+1
690 RETURN
```

The program NEURON4P implements these ideas and calculates the inner product of a vector with a matrix. This simple program is not too useful by itself; but it will be used to build other programs. A simplified flow diagram of the program logic is shown in Fig. 3-3. This brief flow chart shows that after the T matrix is filled the input vector, u, is filled, and the inner product is found between the T matrix and vector u. After vector v is computed, vectors

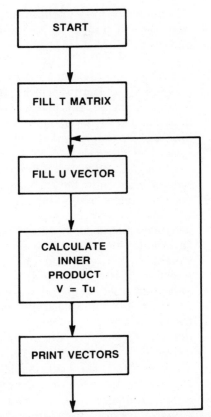

Fig. 3-3. General flow chart for program NEURONXP.

u and v are printed to the line printer. Then a new u vector is selected and the process starts all over again.

Let's examine the program in more detail. In lines 10-20 a randomized seed is entered. In most digital computers the random number generator needs a seed. Often the seed number can be generated by the timer. If the operator has control of the seed then the same random number sequence is always generated. This is convenient for testing and developing programs. In line 40 the number of neurons, N, is entered. A maximum has been set at 100 in the DIM statement of line 90. This can be changed as desired by the user.

Continuing with the theory. Recall Fig. 2-7 defines the threshold value, I_t from the equation

$$V_i = \begin{cases} 1 \text{ if } \sum_j T_{ij} u_j + I_{info} > I_T \\ 0 \text{ otherwise} \end{cases}$$

The output of the ith neuron is logic 1 if the sum of the products of the elements $T_{ij}u_j$ and I_{info} is greater than the threshold voltage, otherwise the output is logic 0.

The threshold is input in line 50 as variable IO. For small networks it is sufficient to choose 0 or 1 for the threshold. This is equivalent to shifting the curve of Fig. 2-7 to the left or right. The information input to the neuron is entered in line 60. This information to the neuron can be thought of as a bias from another signal source and/or noise. It is simply called INFO in the program. By experimenting with the INFO and IO variables the user can get very different results.

Lines 70 and 80 ask if the user would like to enter the input vector and synapse matrix from the keyboard or have the program select a random binary vector for input and a random, dilute, symmetric matrix with $T_{ii} = 0$.

Line 110 is a decision point for an operator-entered T matrix or a machine-generated matrix. Lines 120-170 allow the user to enter the matrix from the keyboard. Lines 190-350 are for a machine-generated matrix. A random variable R, between 0 and 1 is selected in line 210. Line 220 dilutes the selection. If $R < 0.75$ then $R = 0$ else $R = +1$. The T_{ij} element being addressed is set equal to this R value in line 230. At the completion of line 260 the matrix is now filled and dilute. Line 270 begins a routine to diagonalize the matrix and in line 290, T_{ii} is set to zero. Line 300 symmetrizes the matrix with $T_{ij} = T_{ji}$. Finally in line 310 the matrix is printed out to the line printer.

In line 360 the process to fill the input vector, u, is started. If the operator chooses to enter the vector from the keyboard, then lines 380-410 are executed; otherwise, the machine selects a random binary vector in lines 430-460. This routine calls the subroutine in lines 670-690, to select a random number and decide if the vector element should be a 0 or a 1.

In line 470 the calculation of the inner product of the input vector and the T matrix is started. In line 500 the variable named SIGMA is assigned to the result of this calculation. To this SIGMA value is added the INFO value in line 520. Finally in line 530, SIGMA is compared with the threshold value IO and set equal to 0 or 1, depending on results. This final result becomes output vector element v_i. After the v vector is filled by calculations, the u vector and v vector are sent to the line printer in lines 580 and 620. In line 660 the process continues by selecting a new input vector u. The program will end only by a BREAK.

Now that this program has been discussed in detail I can move on to other programs. Table 3-1 summarizes the programs and their differences. These will be explained in a little more detail by the Table.

Table 3-1. Programs and Their Functions Used in This Text.

Program	Comments
NEURON4P	Basic program to find inner product of a vector and a matrix. $T_{ij} = T_{ji}$ and $T_{ii} = 0$
NEURON5P	Same as NEURON4P but matrix is random and a little more dilute. $T_{ij} \# T_{ji}$
NEURON6P	Iterated version of NEURON5P. Eight iterations then prints resulting vector.
NEURON8P	Includes energy calculations between each iteration.
HEBB2P	One memory vector.
HEBB3P	m memory vectors.

The next program to be examined is NEURON5P. With this program you can see the effects of a random dilute matrix. In line 210 the random element is chosen, and in line 220 the matrix is diluted. In this program the matrix will be more dilute than in NEURON4P. In this program if R < 0.85 then R = 0, otherwise R is set equal to +1. This results in less than 15 percent of the elements being set to 1. In NEURON4P the dilution was 25 percent. The rest of this program is similar to NEURON4P.

NEURON5P

```
10 CLS
20 INPUT "INPUT RANDOM SEED ";SEED
30 RANDOMIZE SEED
40 INPUT "ENTER THE NUMBER OF NEURONS (100 MAXIMUM) ";N
50 INPUT "INPUT THE THRESHOLD VALUE (0 TO 2 ARE REASONABLE
VALUES) ";IO
60 INPUT "ENTER THE VALUE OF THE INFORMATION (0 TO 1 IS A GOOD
VALUE) ";INFO
70 INPUT "DO YOU WANT TO ENTER THE INPUT VECTOR YOURSELF
(1/YES, 0/NO)? ";VECTOR
80 INPUT "DO YOU WANT TO INPUT THE T MATRIX (1/Y 0/NO)
";MATRIX
90 DIM T(100,100),V(100),U(100)
100 REM FILL T(I,J) MATRIX
110 IF MATRIX=0 THEN 190
120 FOR I=1 TO N
130 FOR J=1 TO N
140 PRINT "T(";I;",";J;") "
150 INPUT T(I,J)
160 NEXT J
```

```
170 NEXT I
180 GOTO 360 : 'FILL INPUT VECTOR
190 FOR I=1 TO N
200 FOR J=1 TO N
210 R=RND(1)
220 IF R<.85 THEN R=0 ELSE R=+1 : REM DILUTE MATRIX
230 T(I,J)=R
240 NEXT J
250 LPRINT
260 NEXT I
270 FOR I=1 TO N
280 FOR J=1 TO N
290 IF I=J THEN T(I,J)=0
300 REM  T(J,I)=T(I,J)
310 LPRINT T(I,J);
320 NEXT J
330 LPRINT
340 NEXT I
350 LPRINT : LPRINT : LPRINT
360 REM FILL INPUT VECTOR U
370 IF VECTOR=0 THEN 430
380 FOR I=1 TO N
390 PRINT "INPUT U(";I;")"
400 INPUT U(I)
410 NEXT I
420 GOTO 470 : 'BEGIN CALCULATIONS OF OUTPUT VECTOR
430 FOR I=1 TO N
440 GOSUB 670
450 U(I)=R
460 NEXT I
470 REM BEGIN CALCULATION
480 FOR I=1 TO N
490 FOR J=1 TO N
500 SIGMA=T(I,J)*U(J)+SIGMA
510 NEXT J
520 SIGMA=SIGMA+INFO
530 IF SIGMA > IO THEN SIGMA=1 ELSE SIGMA=0
540 U(I)=SIGMA
550 SIGMA=0
560 NEXT I
570 FOR I=1 TO N
580 LPRINT U(I);
590 NEXT I
600 LPRINT : LPRINT
610 FOR I=1 TO N
620 LPRINT U(I);
630 NEXT I
640 LPRINT : LPRINT
```

```
650 LPRINT:LPRINT
660 GOTO 360
670 R=RND(1)
680 IF R<.5 THEN R=0 ELSE R=+1
690 RETURN
```

A run of this program will produce some stable states but it also produces many spurious states. Stable states can be thought of as low points on an energy hyperplane in an n-dimensional hypercube. This will be explained more clearly later in this chapter. It is interesting to note that a run of program NEURON5P results in some spurious states. There are two problems. One is that the matrix is nonsymmetric. The second is that iterative dynamics have not been implemented in this program. By iterative dynamics I mean that the results from one vector-matrix product should be sent back into the network and operated on again by the same matrix. Only by iterative operation can these massively parallel networks compute stable states. As pointed out in Chapter 2, the neurons or threshold logic processors are connected to each other through a synapse or conductance matrix. The output of a processor can be connected to the input of several other processors. Each threshold logic device sums the inputs it receives. The signal travels around this feedback loop, but not to itself, many times in a second before the stable state is reached. Iterative dynamics have been introduced in the next program.

NEURON6P

```
10 CLS
20 INPUT "INPUT RANDOM SEED ";SEED
30 RANDOMIZE SEED
40 INPUT "ENTER THE NUMBER OF NEURONS (100 MAXIMUM) ";N
50 INPUT "INPUT THE THRESHOLD VALUE (0 TO 2 ARE REASONABLE
VALUES) ";I0
60 INPUT "ENTER THE VALUE OF THE INFORMATION (0 TO 1 IS A GOOD
VALUE) ";INFO
70 INPUT "DO YOU WANT TO ENTER THE INPUT VECTOR YOURSELF
(1/YES, 0/NO)? ";VECTOR
80 INPUT "DO YOU WANT TO INPUT THE T MATRIX (1/Y 0/NO)
";MATRIX
90 DIM T(100,100),V(100),U(100)
100 REM FILL T(I,J) MATRIX
110 IF MATRIX=0 THEN 190
120 FOR I=1 TO N
130 FOR J=1 TO N
140 PRINT "T(";I;",";J;") "
150 INPUT T(I,J)
160 NEXT J
170 NEXT I
```

```
180 GOTO 360 : 'FILL INPUT VECTOR
190 FOR I-1 TO N
200 FOR J-1 TO N
210 R-RND(1)
220 IF R<.8 THEN R-0 ELSE R-+1 : REM DILUTE MATRIX
230 T(I,J)-R
240 NEXT J
250 LPRINT
260 NEXT I
270 FOR I-1 TO N
280 FOR J-1 TO N
290 IF I-J THEN T(I,J)-0
300 T(J,I)-T(I,J)
310 LPRINT T(I,J);
320 NEXT J
330 LPRINT
340 NEXT I
350 LPRINT : LPRINT : LPRINT
360 REM FILL INPUT VECTOR U
370 IF VECTOR-0 THEN 430
380 FOR I-1 TO N
390 PRINT "INPUT U(";I;")"
400 INPUT U(I)
410 NEXT I
420 GOTO 470 : 'BEGIN CALCULATIONS OF OUTPUT VECTOR
430 FOR I-1 TO N
440 GOSUB 720
450 U(I)-R
460 NEXT I
470 REM BEGIN CALCULATION
480 FOR ITERATE-1 TO 8 : REM THIS ALLOWS THE OUTPUT VECTOR TO
BE FEED BACK
490 FOR I-1 TO N
500 FOR J-1 TO N
510 SIGMA-T(I,J)*U(J)+SIGMA
520 NEXT J
530 SIGMA-SIGMA+INFO
540 IF SIGMA > IO THEN SIGMA-1 ELSE SIGMA-0
550 U(I)-SIGMA
560 SIGMA-0
570 NEXT I
580 IF ITERATE-1 THEN 590 ELSE 630
590 FOR I-1 TO N
600 LPRINT U(I);
610 NEXT I
620 LPRINT
630 FOR I-1 TO N
640 U(I)-V(I) : REM FOR FEEDBACK
```

```
650 NEXT I
660 NEXT ITERATE
670 FOR I=1 TO N
680 LPRINT V(I);
690 NEXT I
700 LPRINT:LPRINT:LPRINT:LPRINT
710 GOTO 360
720 R=RND(1)
730 IF R<.5 THEN R=0 ELSE R=+1
740 RETURN
```

In NEURON6P a new variable, ITERATE, has been introduced. This variable is a counter in a loop that starts in line 480. The output vector from the inner product of the input vector and the matrix is set equal to a new input vector in line 640. The inner product of this vector and the matrix is then found and the process repeated eight times. Later you will see that eight times is a few too many. Only 3 to 4 times is needed. This program prints the matrix. Then it prints the initial input vector followed by the eighth iterated resulting vector as the output. A new initial vector is then selected and the process started over again. A run of this program is shown in Fig. 3-4.

Notice there still appears to be more than one stable state. From Table 2-1 you know that for an eight-neuron circuit you can have only one stable state. This can be explained from an energy consideration. By the iterative dynamics the algorithm computes the minimal states in an n-dimensional hyperspace. By definition there will be more than one minimum on this hypersurface. In fact, all the corners of the hypercube are stable states. These do not all have the same degree of stability and might only be metastable states. These minima are strange attractors. Although the Lorentz system shown in Fig. 3-5 (Abraham & Shaw, 1984) has two strange attracting points they are not energy surface attracting points, but they are examples of strange attractors. A convenient way of thinking about the energy surface is like a sheet of rubber being pulled in many directions, from many points on its surface. This results in a surface with hills, valleys and wells. If a small marble is dropped on this surface it will be attracted to the nearest, lowest point. This point might not be the lowest point in the entire hypersurface, it is just a local minima or attractor. If the marble is kicked around hard enough it will jump out of this local minima and settle to the next. Repeating this process will result in the marble settling in the deepest basin of attraction. This is the most stable memory state of the network.

MATRIX

```
O O O O O O O 1
O O 1 O O O O O
O 1 O O O O O O
O O O O O 1 O O
O O O O O O O O
O O O 1 O O O O
O O O O O O O 1
1 O O O O O 1 O
```

Input 1	O	O	O	1	O	1	1	O	**Input 12**	O	1	1	1	1	1	1	O
Output 1	1	O	O	1	O	1	1	O	**Output 12**	1	1	1	1	O	1	1	O
Input 2	O	O	O	O	1	1	O	1	**Input 13**	1	1	O	O	O	O	O	1
Output 2	O	O	O	O	O	1	O	1	**Output 13**	1	1	O	O	O	O	1	1
Input 3	O	O	1	O	O	1	O	O	**Input 14**	1	O	1	O	O	O	O	O
Output 3	O	O	1	O	O	1	O	O	**Output 14**	1	O	1	O	O	O	1	O
Input 4	1	O	1	O	1	1	O	1	**Input 15**	1	1	O	1	O	O	1	1
Output 4	1	O	1	O	O	1	1	1	**Output 15**	1	1	O	1	O	O	1	1
Input 5	O	1	1	O	O	O	1	1	**Input 16**	1	O	1	O	O	O	1	1
Output 5	1	1	1	O	O	O	1	1	**Output 16**	1	O	1	O	O	O	1	1
Input 6	1	1	1	O	O	1	1	O	**Input 17**	1	1	1	1	1	1	1	O
Output 6	1	1	1	O	O	1	1	O	**Output 17**	1	1	1	1	O	1	1	O
Input 7	O	O	1	1	O	1	O	1	**Input 18**	O	1	O	O	O	O	O	1
Output 7	O	O	1	1	O	1	O	1	**Output 18**	O	1	O	O	O	O	O	1
Input 8	O	1	O	1	1	1	1	1	**Input 19**	1	O	1	O	1	O	O	O
Output 8	1	1	O	1	O	1	1	1	**Output 19**	1	O	1	O	O	O	1	O
Input 9	O	1	O	1	O	O	O	1	**Input 20**	O	O	1	1	O	O	1	1
Output 9	O	1	O	1	O	O	O	1	**Output 20**	1	O	1	1	O	O	1	1
Input 10	O	1	O	O	O	1	1	1	**Input 21**	1	1	O	1	O	O	1	1
Output 10	1	1	O	O	O	1	1	1	**Output 21**	1	1	O	1	O	O	1	1
Input 11	1	O	1	1	O	1	1	O	**Input 22**	1	O	1	O	O	1	O	1
Output 11	1	O	1	1	O	1	1	O	**Output 22**	1	O	1	O	O	1	1	1

Fig. 3-4. Example run of program NEURON6P. Seed 72873, threshold 1, information 1.

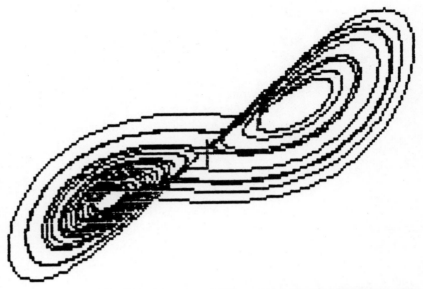

Fig. 3-5. Example of strange attractor. Lorentz curves with two attracting points.

The computed result shows several minima. In Chapter 4 we will build a circuit with physical components. Because of Johnson noise and other component noise you will see that only one stable state results for an eight-neuron circuit. This noise is the analogous effect of kicking the marble around until it settles in the deepest basin of attraction.

The next program calculates the energy after each iteration. Goles and Vichniac (1986) give the energy calculation for a Hopfield (1982, 1984) model as

$$E(t) = -\tfrac{1}{2} \sum_{i=1}^{N} V_i^{t+1} \sum_{j=1}^{N} T_{ij} V_j^t$$

What this algorithm says is that the inner product of vector v at time t, with connection strength matrix T, is multiplied with the vector v at time t + 1. Let time t count the number of sweeps through the network and t + 1 is the next sweep. This second multiplication is an inner product of two vectors and results in a scalar. This scalar value is proportional to the energy. From this dynamic equation it is clear that the energy reaches a minimum when:

$$\sum_{i}^{N} V_i^{t+1} = \sum_{j}^{N} T_{ij} V_j^t$$

This is clearly seen in a computer simulation. After a few iterations, usually four or less, the energy settles to a stable point. Now let us examine the program, NEURON8P.

NEURON8P

```
10 CLS
20 INPUT "INPUT RANDOM SEED ";SEED
30 RANDOMIZE SEED
40 INPUT "ENTER THE NUMBER OF NEURONS (100 MAXIMUM) ";N
50 INPUT "INPUT THE THRESHOLD VALUE (0 TO 2 ARE REASONABLE
VALUES) ";IO
60 INPUT "ENTER THE VALUE OF THE INFORMATION (0 TO 1 IS A GOOD
VALUE) ";INFO
70 INPUT "DO YOU WANT TO ENTER THE INPUT VECTOR YOURSELF
(1/YES, 0/NO)? ";VECTOR
80 INPUT "DO YOU WANT TO INPUT THE T MATRIX (1/Y 0/NO)
";MATRIX
90 DIM T(100,100),V(100),U(100)
100 REM FILL T(I,J) MATRIX
110 IF MATRIX=0 THEN 190
120 FOR I=1 TO N
130 FOR J=1 TO N
140 PRINT "T(";I;",";J;") "
150 INPUT T(I,J)
160 NEXT J
170 NEXT I
180 GOTO 360 : 'FILL INPUT VECTOR
190 FOR I=1 TO N
200 FOR J=1 TO N
210 R=RND(1)
220 IF R<.8 THEN R=0 ELSE R=+1 : REM DILUTE MATRIX
230 T(I,J)=R
240 NEXT J
250 LPRINT
260 NEXT I
270 FOR I=1 TO N
280 FOR J=1 TO N
290 IF I=J THEN T(I,J)=0
300 T(J,I)=T(I,J)
310 LPRINT T(I,J);
320 NEXT J
330 LPRINT
340 NEXT I
350 LPRINT:LPRINT:LPRINT
360 REM FILL INPUT VECTOR U
370 IF VECTOR=0 THEN 430
380 FOR I=1 TO N
390 PRINT "INPUT U(";I;")"
400 INPUT U(I)
410 NEXT I
420 GOTO 470 : 'BEGIN CALCULATIONS OF OUTPUT VECTOR
```

```
430 FOR I-1 TO N
440 GOSUB 790
450 U(I)-R
460 NEXT I
470 REM BEGIN CALCULATION
480 FOR ITERATE-1 TO 8 : REM THIS ALLOWS THE OUTPUT VECTOR TO
BE FEED BACK
490 FOR I-1 TO N
500 FOR J-1 TO N
510 SIGMA-T(I,J)*U(J)+SIGMA
520 NEXT J
530 SIGMA-SIGMA+INFO
540 IF SIGMA > IO THEN SIGMA-1 ELSE SIGMA-0
550 U(I)-SIGMA
560 SIGMA-0
570 NEXT I
580 FOR I-1 TO N
590 LPRINT U(I);
600 NEXT I
610 LPRINT
620 FOR I-1 TO N
630 LPRINT V(I);
640 NEXT I
650 LPRINT
660 ENERGY-0
670 FOR I-1 TO N : REM ENERGY CALCULATION
680 ENERGY-ENERGY+(U(I)*V(I))
690 NEXT I
700 ENERGY--.5*ENERGY
710 LPRINT " ENERGY ";ENERGY : PRINT
720 FOR I-1 TO N
730 U(I)-V(I) : REM FOR FEEDBACK
740 NEXT I
750 ENERGY-0
760 NEXT ITERATE
770 LPRINT : LPRINT : LPRINT : LPRINT
780 GOTO 360
790 R-RND(1)
800 IF R<.5 THEN R-0 ELSE R-+1
810 RETURN
```

The program NEURON8P introduces the new variable ENERGY. The energy calculation takes place within the ITERATE loop. The energy is set equal to zero in line 660, calculations take place in a loop starting at 670, and ending at 690. The final energy is printed out in line 700. In line 750 the energy is set equal to zero again, and the next iteration begins. Figure 3-6 shows a run of this program. After the matrix is printed the random binary vector is printed,

MATRIX

```
O  O  O  O  1  O  O  O  O  O  1  1  O  O  O  O
O  O  O  O  O  O  O  O  O  O  O  1  O  O  O  O
O  O  O  O  O  O  1  O  O  O  O  O  1  O  O  1
O  O  O  O  O  O  O  O  1  O  1  O  O  O  O  O
1  O  O  O  O  1  O  O  O  1  O  O  O  O  1  1
O  O  O  O  1  O  O  O  O  O  O  O  O  O  O  O
O  O  1  O  O  O  O  O  O  O  O  1  O  O  O  O
O  O  O  O  O  O  O  O  1  O  1  1  O  1  O  O
O  O  O  1  O  O  O  1  O  O  O  1  O  1  O  1
O  O  O  O  1  O  O  O  O  O  1  1  O  O  O  O
1  O  O  1  O  O  O  1  O  1  O  O  O  O  O  1
1  1  O  O  O  O  1  1  1  1  O  O  O  O  O  O
O  O  1  O  O  O  O  O  O  O  O  O  O  O  O  1
O  O  O  O  O  O  O  1  1  O  O  O  O  O  O  O
O  O  O  O  1  O  O  O  O  O  O  O  O  O  O  O
O  O  1  O  1  O  O  O  1  O  1  O  1  O  O  O
```

Input 1	1	O	1	O	1	O	1	1	1	1	O	1	1	O	O	O
Output 1	1	O	1	O	1	O	1	1	1	1	1	1	O	1	O	1
			ENERGY −4													
Input 2	1	O	1	O	1	O	1	1	1	1	1	1	O	1	O	1
Output 2	1	O	1	1	1	O	1	1	1	1	1	1	1	1	O	1
			ENERGY −5.5													
Input 3	1	O	1	1	1	O	1	1	1	1	1	1	1	1	O	1
Output 3	1	O	1	1	1	O	1	1	1	1	1	1	1	1	O	1
			ENERGY −6.5													
Input 4	1	O	1	1	1	O	1	1	1	1	1	1	1	1	O	1
Output 4	1	O	1	1	1	O	1	1	1	1	1	1	1	1	O	1
			ENERGY −6.5													
Input 5	1	O	1	1	1	O	1	1	1	1	1	1	1	1	O	1
Output 5	1	O	1	1	1	O	1	1	1	1	1	1	1	1	O	1
			ENERGY −6.5													
Input 6	1	O	1	1	1	O	1	1	1	1	1	1	1	1	O	1
Output 6	1	O	1	1	1	O	1	1	1	1	1	1	1	1	O	1
			ENERGY −6.5													
Input 7	1	O	1	1	1	O	1	1	1	1	1	1	1	1	O	1
Output 7	1	O	1	1	1	O	1	1	1	1	1	1	1	1	O	1
			ENERGY −6.5													
Input 8	1	O	1	1	1	O	1	1	1	1	1	1	1	1	O	1
Output 8	1	O	1	1	1	O	1	1	1	1	1	1	1	1	O	1
			ENERGY −6.5													

Fig. 3-6. Example run of program NEURON8P. Seed 0, threshold 1, information 0.

```
Input 9    1  O  1  1  1  O  1  O  1  1  O  1  O  1  1  1
Output 9   1  O  1  O  1  O  1  1  1  1  1  1  1  O  O  1
                ENERGY  -4
Input 10   1  O  1  O  1  O  1  1  1  1  1  1  1  O  O  1
Output 10  1  O  1  1  1  O  1  1  1  1  1  1  1  1  O  1
                ENERGY  -5.5
Input 11   1  O  1  1  1  O  1  1  1  1  1  1  1  1  O  1
Output 11  1  O  1  1  1  O  1  1  1  1  1  1  1  1  O  1
                ENERGY  -6.5
Input 12   1  O  1  1  1  O  1  1  1  1  1  1  1  1  O  1
Output 12  1  O  1  1  1  O  1  1  1  1  1  1  1  1  O  1
                ENERGY  -6.5
Input 13   1  O  1  1  1  O  1  1  1  1  1  1  1  1  O  1
Output 13  1  O  1  1  1  O  1  1  1  1  1  1  1  1  O  1
                ENERGY  -6.5
Input 14   1  O  1  1  1  O  1  1  1  1  1  1  1  1  O  1
Output 14  1  O  1  1  1  O  1  1  1  1  1  1  1  1  O  1
                ENERGY  -6.5
Input 15   1  O  1  1  1  O  1  1  1  1  1  1  1  1  O  1
Output 15  1  O  1  1  1  O  1  1  1  1  1  1  1  1  O  1
                ENERGY  -6.5
Input 16   1  O  1  1  1  O  1  1  1  1  1  1  1  1  O  1
Output 16  1  O  1  1  1  O  1  1  1  1  1  1  1  1  O  1
                ENERGY  -6.5


Input 17   1  1  O  1  1  1  O  O  1  1  O  O  O  1  O  O
Output 17  O  O  O  O  1  O  O  1  1  O  1  1  O  O  O  1
                ENERGY  -1
Input 18   O  O  O  O  1  O  O  1  1  O  1  1  O  O  O  1
Output 18  1  O  O  1  O  O  O  1  1  1  1  1  O  1  O  1
                ENERGY  -2.5
Input 19   1  O  O  1  O  O  O  1  1  1  1  1  O  1  O  1
Output 19  1  O  O  1  1  O  O  1  1  1  1  1  O  1  O  1
                ENERGY  -4.5
Input 20   1  O  O  1  1  O  O  1  1  1  1  1  O  1  O  1
Output 20  1  O  O  1  1  O  O  1  1  1  1  1  O  1  O  1
                ENERGY  -5
Input 21   1  O  O  1  1  O  O  1  1  1  1  1  O  1  O  1
Output 21  1  O  O  1  1  O  O  1  1  1  1  1  O  1  O  1
                ENERGY  -5
Input 22   1  O  O  1  1  O  O  1  1  1  1  1  O  1  O  1
Output 22  1  O  O  1  1  O  O  1  1  1  1  1  O  1  O  1
                ENERGY  -5
Input 23   1  O  O  1  1  O  O  1  1  1  1  1  O  1  O  1
Output 23  1  O  O  1  1  O  O  1  1  1  1  1  O  1  O  1
                ENERGY  -5
Input 24   1  O  O  1  1  O  O  1  1  1  1  1  O  1  O  1
Output 24  1  O  O  1  1  O  O  1  1  1  1  1  O  1  O  1
                ENERGY  -5
```

then, the resulting inner product vector and energy is printed. The program then begins the next iteration by feeding the resulting vector back into the matrix calculation.

Looking at Fig. 3-6 you see that, in the case of the first random binary vector, the energy has a value of -4 after the first iteration, and -5.5 after the second iteration, finally settling to a stable state at -6.5 energy units. In the next two programs we will examine associative learning using the Hebb learning rule.

ASSOCIATIVE LEARNING: THE HEBB LEARNING RULE

The program HEBB2P is a basic building unit for the Hebb learning rule. This rule was introduced in Chapter 2 and will be reiterated here. The original Hebb learning rule (Hebb, 1949) was not quantitative enough to build a good model. The rule in its original version stated that if neuron A and neuron B are simultaneously excited then the synaptic connection strength between them is increased.

HEBB2P

```
10 CLS
20 INPUT "INPUT RANDOM SEED ";SEED
30 RANDOMIZE SEED
40 INPUT "ENTER THE NUMBER OF NEURONS (100 MAXIMUM) ";N
50 INPUT "INPUT THE THRESHOLD VALUE (0 TO 2 ARE REASONABLE
VALUES) ";I0
60 INPUT "ENTER THE VALUE OF THE INFORMATION (0 TO 1 IS A GOOD
VALUE) ";INFO
70 INPUT "DO YOU WANT TO ENTER THE INPUT VECTOR YOURSELF
(1/YES 0/NO)? ";VECTOR
80 PRINT "BINARY MATRIX WITH TII-0 AND TIJ-TJI ."
90 DIM T(100,100),V(100),U(100)
100 REM FILL T(I,J) MATRIX
110 PRINT:PRINT:PRINT
120 PRINT "INPUT THE MEMORY VECTOR FOR THE HEBB MATRIX"
130 FOR I-1 TO N
140 PRINT "V(";I;")"
150 INPUT V(I)
160 U(I)-V(I)
170 NEXT I
180 FOR I-1 TO N
190 FOR J-1 TO N
200 T(I,J)-V(I)*U(J)
210 IF I-J THEN T(I,J)-0
220 LPRINT T(I,J);
230 NEXT J
```

```
240 LPRINT
250 NEXT I
260 LPRINT : LPRINT : LPRINT
270 REM FILL INPUT VECTOR U
280 IF VECTOR-0 THEN 340
290 FOR I-1 TO N
300 PRINT "INPUT U(" ; I ; ")"
310 INPUT U(I)
320 NEXT I
330 GOTO 380 : 'BEGIN CALCULATIONS OF OUTPUT VECTOR
340 FOR I-1 TO N
350 GOSUB 630
360 U(I)-R
370 NEXT I
380 REM BEGIN CALCULATION
390 FOR ITERATE-1 TO 8 : REM THIS ALLOWS THE OUTPUT VECTOR TO
BE FEED BACK
400 FOR I-1 TO N
410 FOR J-1 TO N
420 SIGMA-T(I,J)*U(J)+SIGMA
430 NEXT J
440 SIGMA-SIGMA+INFO
450 IF SIGMA > IO THEN SIGMA-1 ELSE SIGMA-0
460 V(I)-SIGMA
470 SIGMA-0
480 NEXT I
490 IF ITERATE-1 THEN 500 ELSE 540
500 FOR I-1 TO N
510 LPRINT U(I) ;
520 NEXT I
530 LPRINT
540 FOR I-1 TO N
550 U(I)-V(I) : REM FOR FEEDBACK
560 NEXT I
570 NEXT ITERATE
580 FOR I-1 TO N
590 LPRINT V(I) ;
600 NEXT I
610 LPRINT : LPRINT : LPRINT : LPRINT
620 GOTO 270
630 R-RND(1)
640 IF R < .5 THEN R-0 ELSE R-+1
650 RETURN
```

An excellent example of associative learning in humans is when we hold a red apple in front of a baby and repeatedly say red. Synaptic connection strengths will be increased when the appropriate neurons from the optic center are simultaneously activated with those from the auditory center for the sound of the word. Another example is Pavlov's experiments in which, after repeated trials, a dog learned to associate the sound of a bell with food. Using this learning rule we could train a simple network such as that shown in Fig. 3-7. An input vector would be presented to both the auditory and optic neurons. The appropriate synaptic connections would then be strengthened.

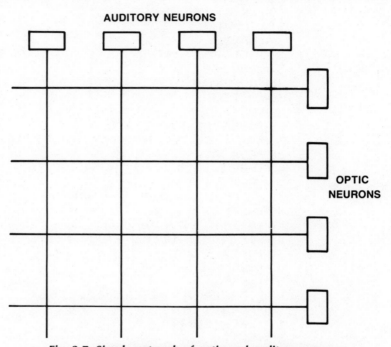

AUDITORY NEURONS

OPTIC NEURONS

Fig. 3-7. Simple network of optic and auditory neurons.

In digital simulations of this model, the outer product of two vectors is found to produce a synaptic connection strength matrix. From Chapter 2 this is given symbolically as:

$$W = u\ v^t$$

For a one dimensional vector of length four, we would get the matrix W.

$$u = [3\ 1\ 2\ 4]$$
$$v = [0\ 1\ 1\ 6]$$

$$W = [3\ 1\ 2\ 4] \begin{bmatrix} 0 \\ 1 \\ 1 \\ 6 \end{bmatrix} = \begin{bmatrix} 0 & 0 & 0 & 0 \\ 3 & 1 & 2 & 4 \\ 3 & 1 & 2 & 4 \\ 18 & 6 & 12 & 24 \end{bmatrix}$$

Notice that I used the transpose of the vector v. Symbolically, to find an element of the matrix you write:

$$W_{ij} = u_i \, v_j^t$$

The connection strengths are the elements of the matrix. These represent the stored memory state or states. If the storage matrix is small only one memory state can be stored. For larger storage matrices, more than one memory can be stored. In this case each memory state will generate one matrix.

$$W^s = u^s \, (v^t)^s \qquad \text{state } s$$

To store all the memories in one matrix the matrices are added over all states.

$$W = \sum W^s$$
$$\text{all states}$$

Table 2-1 summarized the number of memories versus number of neurons. In order to recover the memory state from the storage matrix the inner product of a partial memory and the memory matrix is calculated.

Ideally, the storage matrix would not have just 1's and 0's as exemplified in Chapter 2, rather, it would have + and − numbers varying over a range of values depending on the connection strength of the synapse. Because it is much harder to implement this idea in hardware for artificial neural networks, we use a two-state or binary-strength matrix in the computer simulations. This is why binary model examples were given in Chapter 2. In Chapter 4 with circuit implementations, the matrix will have only one size resistor to represent a 1 and no resistor to represent a 0. Another point is that I will use only symmetric matrices because a nonsymmetric matrix will result in spurious states and chaotic oscillations. For a symmetric matrix you find the outer product of the input vector and its transpose.

Let us discuss the program HEBB2P. Figure 3-8 is a simplified flow diagram of the program logic. The first observation is that there is no END. In order to end, the BREAK key must be pressed. Another obvious observation is that only one memory state is stored in this matrix. This program will be used to develop the next program, HEBB3P, which can store m memory states for N neurons.

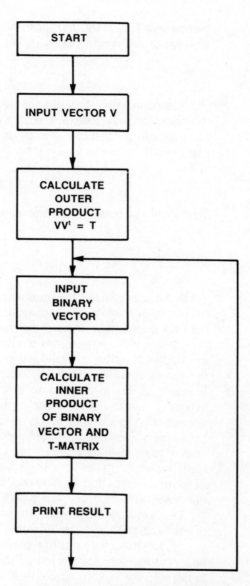

Fig. 3-8. Flow chart for program HEBBXP.

Looking at the program line by line, you see that the memory state is entered in lines 130 to 170. In line 160 the transpose is found by changing the label. Beginning in line 180 the T matrix is filled by finding the outer product of the desired storage vector and its transpose. Line 210 puts 0's on the diagonal of the matrix and line 220 prints the T matrix at the line printer. The rest of the program is exactly like earlier programs. A random binary vector is filled. The inner product of this vector with the T matrix is calculated. This calculation is iterated eight times and the random vector and final product vector are printed at the line printer.

HEBB3P

```
10 CLS
20 INPUT "INPUT RANDOM SEED ";SEED
30 RANDOMIZE SEED
40 INPUT "ENTER THE NUMBER OF NEURONS (100 MAXIMUM) ";N
50 INPUT "DO YOU WANT TO ENTER THE INPUT VECTOR YOURSELF
(1/YES 0/NO)? ";VECTOR
60 DIM T(100,100),V(100),U(100)
70 REM FILL T(I,J) MATRIX
80 PRINT:PRINT:PRINT
90 INPUT "INPUT THE NUMBER OF MEMORY VECTORS (M-INT(.15*N)
";M
100 FOR MEMS-1 TO M
110 PRINT "INPUT THE MEMORY VECTOR ";MEMS;"FOR THE HEBB
MATRIX."
120 FOR I-1 TO N
130 PRINT "V(";I;")"
140 INPUT V(I)
150 U(I)-V(I)
160 NEXT I
170 FOR I-1 TO N
180 FOR J-1 TO N
190 T(I,J)-T(I,J)+V(I)*V(J)
200 IF I-J THEN T(I,J)-0
210 IF T(I,J)>1 THEN T(I,J)-1
220 LPRINT T(I,J);
230 NEXT J
240 LPRINT
250 NEXT I
255 LPRINT:LPRINT:LPRINT
260 NEXT MEMS
270 LPRINT:LPRINT:LPRINT
280 REM FILL INPUT VECTOR U
290 IF VECTOR-0 THEN 350
300 FOR I-1 TO N
310 PRINT "INPUT U(";I;")"
320 INPUT U(I)
330 NEXT I
340 GOTO 390 : 'BEGIN CALCULATIONS OF OUTPUT VECTOR
350 FOR I-1 TO N
360 GOSUB 640
370 U(I)-R
```

```
380 NEXT I
390 REM BEGIN CALCULATION
400 FOR ITERATE=1 TO 8: REM THIS ALLOWS THE OUTPUT VECTOR TO
BE FEED BACK
410 FOR I=1 TO N
420 FOR J=1 TO N
430 SIGMA=T(I,J)*U(J)+SIGMA
440 NEXT J
450 SIGMA=SIGMA
460 IF SIGMA > 0 THEN SIGMA=1 ELSE SIGMA=0
470 V(I)=SIGMA
480 SIGMA=0
490 NEXT I
500 IF ITERATE=1 THEN 510 ELSE 550
510 FOR I=1 TO N
520 LPRINT U(I);
530 NEXT I
540 LPRINT
550 FOR I=1 TO N
560 U(I)=V(I): REM FOR FEEDBACK
570 NEXT I
580 NEXT ITERATE
590 FOR I=1 TO N
600 LPRINT V(I);
610 NEXT I
620 LPRINT: LPRINT: LPRINT: LPRINT
630 GOTO 280
640 R=RND(1)
650 IF R<.5 THEN R=0 ELSE R=+1
660 RETURN
```

Program HEBB3P includes a routine to allow the user to choose the number of memory states to store. This program asks the user how many neurons are to be simulated. It then asks the user how many memory states are to be stored and reminds the user that the number of memory states stored is given by

$$m = INT(0.15N)$$

where N is the number of neurons. This equation for the number of memories is an empirically derived equation. You can experiment with these programs and deduce more or less the same equation for the number of memory states. After the user enters the first memory vector, the first T matrix is found and printed at the line printer. The next memory vector is entered and the new T matrix is printed. This new T matrix includes the sum of the T matrix for state one and state two. This continues through m memory states. Then a random binary vector is chosen or entered from the keyboard, the inner product of this vector and the summed T matrix is found and printed at the line printer along with the random vector.

Figure 3-9 is a run of this program with 16 neurons and two memory states. The two states entered were:

(1 0 0 0 1 0 0 0 1 0 0 0 1 0 0 0)

(0 1 1 0 0 0 1 1 0 0 0 0 0 1 1 0)

Notice that these states did not come out from random vectors, except twice for the second vector, and once for the first vector. In the other cases the Hamming distance is too great to result in a correct memory state. The end result is a stable spurious state. You see that this same stable spurious state arises many times, indicating that it is probably a deeper energy minima than the two stored states. These spurious states can be caused by overlapping vectors in Hamming space, in other words, too many interconnections among the neurons. Some interesting programming experiments would be to include energy calculations between each iteration and see if there are in fact deeper stable states than the stored memory states. Another experiment would be a study of Hamming distance to see how far off one can be in Hamming space and still "pull in" to one of the stored states.

These problems and other learning rules are current active areas of research in many AI laboratories.

MEMORY STATE 1

```
O  O  O  O  1  O  O  O  1  O  O  O  1  O  O  O
O  O  O  O  O  O  O  O  O  O  O  O  O  O  O  O
O  O  O  O  O  O  O  O  O  O  O  O  O  O  O  O
O  O  O  O  O  O  O  O  O  O  O  O  O  O  O  O
1  O  O  O  O  O  O  O  1  O  O  O  1  O  O  O
O  O  O  O  O  O  O  O  O  O  O  O  O  O  O  O
O  O  O  O  O  O  O  O  O  O  O  O  O  O  O  O
O  O  O  O  O  O  O  O  O  O  O  O  O  O  O  O
1  O  O  O  1  O  O  O  O  O  O  O  1  O  O  O
O  O  O  O  O  O  O  O  O  O  O  O  O  O  O  O
O  O  O  O  O  O  O  O  O  O  O  O  O  O  O  O
O  O  O  O  O  O  O  O  O  O  O  O  O  O  O  O
1  O  O  O  1  O  O  O  1  O  O  O  O  O  O  O
O  O  O  O  O  O  O  O  O  O  O  O  O  O  O  O
O  O  O  O  O  O  O  O  O  O  O  O  O  O  O  O
O  O  O  O  O  O  O  O  O  O  O  O  O  O  O  O
```

Input 1	1	1	O	O	O	1	O	1	1	1	1	1	1	O	1	O
Output 1	1	1	1	O	1	O	1	1	1	O	O	O	1	1	1	O
Input 2	O	1	O	O	1	1	O	1	1	O	O	O	O	1	1	O
Output 2	1	1	1	O	1	O	1	1	1	O	O	O	1	1	1	O
Input 3	1	O	O	O	1	O	1	1	O	O	O	O	1	1	O	O
Output 3	1	1	1	O	1	O	1	1	1	O	O	O	1	1	1	O
Input 4	O	O	O	1	1	1	1	1	O	1	1	1	O	O	1	O
Output 4	1	1	1	O	1	O	1	1	1	O	O	O	1	1	1	O
Input 5	O	O	O	1	O	1	1	O	O	O	O	O	1	1	O	1
Output 5	1	1	1	O	1	O	1	1	1	O	O	O	1	1	1	O
Input 6	O	O	1	O	O	1	O	O	1	O	1	O	1	1	O	1
Output 6	1	1	1	O	1	O	1	1	1	O	O	O	1	1	1	O
Input 7	O	1	1	O	O	O	1	1	1	1	1	O	O	1	1	O
Output 7	1	1	1	O	1	O	1	1	1	O	O	O	1	1	1	O
Input 8	O	O	1	1	O	1	O	1	O	1	O	1	1	1	1	1
Output 8	1	1	1	O	1	O	1	1	1	O	O	O	1	1	1	O
Input 9	O	1	O	1	O	O	O	1	O	1	O	O	O	1	1	1
Output 9	O	1	1	O	O	O	1	1	O	O	O	O	O	1	1	O

Fig. 3-9. Example run of HEBB3P. Seed 72873.

MEMORY STATE 2

```
O  O  O  O  1  O  O  O  1  O  O  O  1  O  O  O
O  O  1  O  O  O  1  1  O  O  O  O  O  O  1  1  O
O  1  O  O  O  O  1  1  O  O  O  O  O  O  1  1  O
O  O  O  O  O  O  O  O  O  O  O  O  O  O  O  O
1  O  O  O  O  O  O  O  1  O  O  O  1  O  O  O
O  O  O  O  O  O  O  O  O  O  O  O  O  O  O  O
O  1  1  O  O  O  O  1  O  O  O  O  O  1  1  O
O  1  1  O  O  O  1  O  O  O  O  O  O  1  1  O
1  O  O  O  1  O  O  O  O  O  O  O  1  O  O  O
O  O  O  O  O  O  O  O  O  O  O  O  O  O  O  O
O  O  O  O  O  O  O  O  O  O  O  O  O  O  O  O
O  O  O  O  O  O  O  O  O  O  O  O  O  O  O  O
1  O  O  O  1  O  O  O  1  O  O  O  O  O  O  O
O  1  1  O  O  O  1  1  O  O  O  O  O  O  1  O
O  1  1  O  O  O  1  1  O  O  O  O  O  1  O  O
O  O  O  O  O  O  O  O  O  O  O  O  O  O  O  O
```

Input 10	1	O	1	1	O	1	1	O	O	1	1	1	1	1	1	O
Output 10	1	1	1	O	1	O	1	1	1	O	O	O	1	1	1	O
Input 11	1	1	O	O	O	O	O	1	1	O	1	O	O	O	O	O
Output 11	1	1	1	O	1	O	1	1	1	O	O	O	1	1	1	O
Input 12	1	1	O	1	O	O	1	1	1	O	1	O	O	O	1	1
Output 12	1	1	1	O	1	O	1	1	1	O	O	O	1	1	1	O
Input 13	1	1	1	1	1	1	1	O	O	1	O	O	O	O	O	1
Output 13	1	1	1	O	1	O	1	1	1	O	O	O	1	1	1	O
Input 14	1	O	1	O	1	O	O	O	O	O	1	1	O	O	1	1
Output 14	1	1	1	O	1	O	1	1	1	O	O	O	1	1	1	O
Input 15	1	1	O	1	O	O	1	1	1	O	1	O	O	1	O	1
Output 15	1	1	1	O	1	O	1	1	1	O	O	O	1	1	1	O
Input 16	1	1	1	1	O	1	O	O	1	1	1	O	O	O	1	O
Output 16	1	1	1	O	1	O	1	1	1	O	O	O	1	1	1	O
Input 17	1	1	1	O	1	1	O	1	O	1	O	O	1	O	1	O
Output 17	1	1	1	O	1	O	1	1	1	O	O	O	1	1	1	O
Input 18	1	1	1	O	1	O	1	O	O	O	O	O	O	1	1	O
Output 18	1	1	1	O	1	O	1	1	1	O	O	O	1	1	1	O

Input 19	1	1	1	1	0	1	0	0	1	0	1	0	0	1	0	0
Output 19	1	1	1	0	1	0	1	1	1	0	0	0	1	1	1	0
Input 20	1	1	1	1	0	0	1	1	1	1	1	0	0	0	1	1
Output 20	1	1	1	0	1	0	1	1	1	0	0	0	1	1	1	0
Input 21	1	0	0	1	1	1	0	0	1	1	0	1	0	0	0	0
Output 21	1	0	0	0	1	0	0	0	1	0	0	0	1	0	0	0
Input 22	1	0	1	0	0	0	0	1	1	1	1	0	1	0	1	0
Output 22	1	1	1	0	1	0	1	1	1	0	0	0	1	1	1	0
Input 23	1	0	1	1	0	0	1	0	1	1	0	1	0	1	1	0
Output 23	1	1	1	0	1	0	1	1	1	0	0	0	1	1	1	0
Input 24	1	1	1	1	1	0	1	1	1	1	1	1	0	0	0	
Output 24	1	1	1	0	1	0	1	1	1	0	0	0	1	1	1	0
Input 25	1	0	0	0	1	1	1	1	1	1	1	0	1	1	1	0
Output 25	1	1	1	0	1	0	1	1	1	0	0	0	1	1	1	0
Input 26	1	0	1	0	1	1	1	1	1	0	0	1	1	1	1	0
Output 26	1	1	1	0	1	0	1	1	1	0	0	0	1	1	1	0
Input 27	1	0	0	0	0	1	0	1	0	0	0	0	0	1	0	1
Output 27	1	1	1	0	1	0	1	1	1	0	0	0	1	1	1	0
Input 28	0	1	1	0	0	0	1	1	0	0	0	0	1	0	1	0
Output 28	1	1	1	0	1	0	1	1	1	0	0	0	1	1	1	0
Input 29	1	1	1	0	0	0	0	1	0	1	0	1	1	0	0	1
Output 29	1	1	1	0	1	0	1	1	1	0	0	0	1	1	1	0
Input 30	0	1	0	0	0	0	0	1	1	1	0	0	0	0	1	0
Output 30	1	1	1	0	1	0	1	1	1	0	0	0	1	1	1	0
Input 31	1	1	0	1	0	0	0	1	0	0	0	0	0	0	1	1
Output 31	1	1	1	0	1	0	1	1	1	0	0	0	1	1	1	0
Input 32	1	1	1	0	1	1	1	0	1	0	1	0	1	0	1	1
Output 32	1	1	1	0	1	0	1	1	1	0	0	0	1	1	1	0

Input 33	O	1	1	1	O	1	O	O	O	1	O	O	O	1	O	O
Output 33	O	1	1	O	O	O	1	1	O	O	O	O	O	O	1	1	O
Input 34	1	O	1	O	O	1	O	O	O	O	1	O	O	1	1	O
Output 34	1	1	1	O	1	O	1	1	1	O	O	O	1	1	1	O
Input 35	O	1	O	1	1	O	O	O	O	O	O	1	O	1	O	O
Output 35	1	1	1	O	1	O	1	1	1	O	O	O	1	1	1	O
Input 36	1	O	O	O	O	1	1	O	O	O	O	1	1	1	O	O
Output 36	1	1	1	O	1	O	1	1	1	O	O	O	1	1	1	O
Input 37	1	O	O	1	O	O	O	1	O	1	O	O	O	O	1	1
Output 37	1	1	1	O	1	O	1	1	1	O	O	O	1	1	1	O
Input 38	1	1	1	1	1	O	O	1	O	O	O	O	O	O	O	1
Output 38	1	1	1	O	1	O	1	1	1	O	O	O	1	1	1	O
Input 39	1	1	1	1	1	O	1	O	1	1	O	1	O	1	O	1
Output 39	1	1	1	O	1	O	1	1	1	O	O	O	1	1	1	O
Input 40	O	1	1	O	O	O	O	1	1	1	1	1	O	O	O	1
Output 40	1	1	1	O	1	O	1	1	1	O	O	O	1	1	1	O
Input 41	O	1	1	O	O	1	O	1	1	O	O	O	1	1	O	1
Output 41	1	1	1	O	1	O	1	1	1	O	O	O	1	1	1	O
Input 42	O	O	1	O	O	O	O	O	1	O	1	O	1	O	O	O
Output 42	1	1	1	O	1	O	1	1	1	O	O	O	1	1	1	O
	O	O	O	1	1	1	1	1	O	1	1	1	1	O	O	O

4

Electronic Neural Networks

This chapter will discuss operational amplifiers and other IC's that can be used as threshold logic processors. The first circuit to be described is a simple flip-flop using threshold logic, followed by, the N-flop and its applications. A neural network circuit that can easily be interfaced to a PC is then described. The results of this experiment and a computer program are discussed. The final circuit is a general-purpose, programmable, electronic neural network. This circuit will be used to construct a content-addressable memory circuit. Results of running this network and a digital computer simulation from a program in Chapter 3 will be discussed. The final section will present ideas for further projects and experiments.

FLIP-FLOP CIRCUITS

As pointed out in earlier chapters, neurons are threshold logic devices. When the sum of the inputs reaches a certain value, the neuron will *fire* or turn on. This is given by the relation:

$$V_i = \begin{cases} 1 \text{ if } \sum_j T_{ij} u_j + I_{info} > I_{threshold} \\ 0 \text{ otherwise} \end{cases}$$

and is shown in Fig. 4-1. This relation is very well modeled by operational amplifiers. Figure 4-2 schematically shows a summing amplifier circuit.

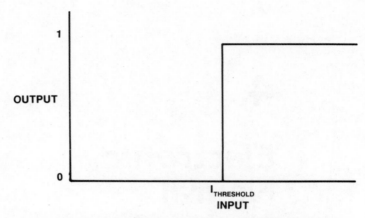

Fig. 4-1. Input/output relation for threshold logic device.

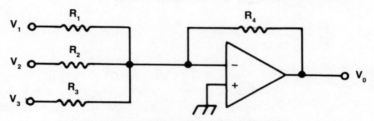

Fig. 4-2. Summing amplifier circuit.

From this circuit we can write Ohm's Law relation for output voltage as:

$$V_0 = - R_4 \left(\frac{V_1}{R_1} + \frac{V_2}{R_2} + \frac{V_3}{R_3} \right)$$

This relation could be extended for summing a large number of analog inputs to the same amplifier. It is significant to note that the circuit described here is an analog circuit. Each amplifier is considered as a processor or threshold logic device in an analog network of parallel processors. Each processor makes a computation or decision based on many analog values from other processors in the network. The analog input to a processor can also come from an information source, such as sensors, set switches, or biased analog voltage.

The first circuit is a flip-flop made from op amps. There are many types of op amps, any of which could be used for analog processing. I prefer to use the LM324A from National Semiconductor. This preference is based on the power requirements for this chip, it can be operated from single or dual power supplies. It is most convenient to operate on +5V, making the chip compatible with CMOS logic power supplies.

When the circuit shown in Fig. 4-3 is constructed, and the outputs are connected to an oscilloscope the following can be observed: If you look at

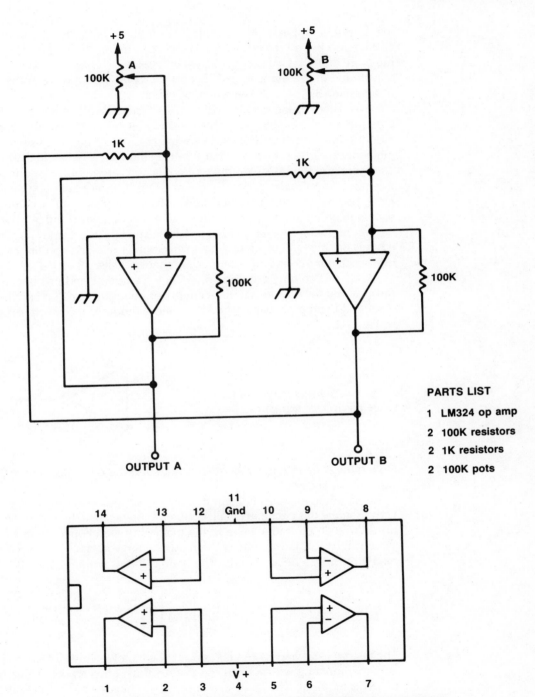

PARTS LIST

1 LM324 op amp
2 100K resistors
2 1K resistors
2 100K pots

Fig. 4-3. Flip-flop from LM324 op amp and pin diagram for LM324.

the output of amplifier A, and adjust the input to amplifier B, you will see an increase in voltage output up to a certain point, then there is a sudden jump in output. Continuing the examination of output A, you see that adjustment of the input A, only affects the baseline. Looking at the output of amplifier B, you will see a similar effect.

We will examine the flip-flop circuits in more detail later in this chapter. One thing interesting to note about this circuit is that the amplifiers are the model neurons or threshold logic processors, and the 1K resistors are the inhibitory synapse connection. Because the amplifiers are used in the inverting configuration, the resistive synapse connections are inhibitory connections. It is possible to make excitatory connections with noninverting amplifiers. Here, use only inhibitory connections. Many complex systems can be modeled with only inhibitory connections. Our model neuron will be a two-state neuron of 0 and 1 value. Other models exist that use -1 and $+1$. The two models are really equivalent with a shift in the operating conditions. When only excitatory connections are used, chaos results.

It is most common to think of CMOS logic buffers and inverters as logic devices. But these buffers and inverters can be used as analog amplifiers for threshold logic processing. The schematic symbol for the inverter is shown in Fig. 4-4.

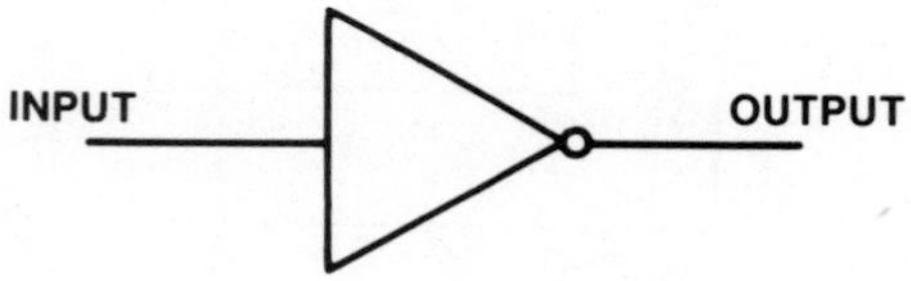

Fig. 4-4. Schematic symbol for the inverter or NOT gate.

INPUT   OUTPUT

Notice the similarity between this symbol and the op amps. This similarity was not an accident.

A simple two-neuron circuit that acts as a flip-flop is shown in Fig. 4-5. Let's examine this circuit in detail. Chapter 3 showed that the synapse resistors needn't be all the same value in the matrix but we clipped them all to the same value. This gave a binary matrix. For energy balance in a flip-flop, the matrix must be a binary matrix. The matrix for this two-processor flip-flop is

$$M = \begin{bmatrix} 0 & 1 \\ 1 & 0 \end{bmatrix}$$

The resistors R21 and R12 in Fig. 4-5 are the matrix elements M21 and M12. By experimenting with various sizes of resistors, one can deduce that 100K to 1M is required. The large size of resistor is needed to give the necessary feedback gain. With R12 = R21 = 100K, the circuit acts as an R-S flip-flop.

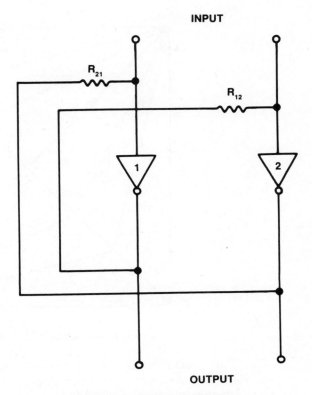

Fig. 4-5. Simple neural flip-flop.

The truth table for this flip-flop is shown in Fig. 4-6. If the system is put in any state determined by the two inputs, then there are two stable output states. This can be thought of as a two-state content-addressable memory. If the input to amplifier A, has a lower analog value than that in amplifier B, then this drives B to a logic 0 or low and A is driven to a logic 1 or high. If you set both inputs high and then "cut the inputs" so the circuit is free-running, you will see that the network will settle to one of the stable states. An energy surface for this network is represented in Fig. 4-7.

In Fig. 4-7, the diagonal line from the upper right corner to the lower left corner represents a ridge on the energy surface. The other lines represent the direction a marble would roll. There are only two stable states. These are corners of the hypercube.

Fig. 4-6. Truth table for flip-flop.

A_{in}	B_{in}	A_{out}	B_{out}
0	1	1	0
1	0	0	1

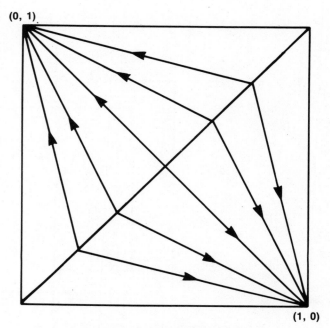

Fig. 4-7. Energy surface for two-neuron flip-flop.

In general, given an N processor network, the state space is an N-dimensional hypercube. For networks with no self connections ($T_{ii} = 0$) and high gain, the corners of the hypercube are the minima. You will see later that this does not necessarily mean that each minima is of equal depth.

PROJECT 1: TWO-PROCESSOR FLIP-FLOP

The first project consists of a two-processor circuit interconnected as a flip-flop. As pointed out earlier, if the amplifiers are allowed to free-run, the network will settle to one of the stable states. This circuit is not actually designed for flip-flop operation, but rather for demonstrating the analog summing behavior of CMOS inverters. The pin diagram for the chips used in this circuit are shown in Fig. 4-8.

The complete circuit is shown in Fig. 4-9 and Photo 4-1. Let us examine the circuit in detail. The two threshold logic processors are 4049 CMOS inverters. These are labeled A and B. The two resistive interconnections are 100K each, as was discussed with Fig. 4-5. We therefore have the same matrix as discussed earlier. The output from the processors are connected to LED's. In addition, the outputs are connected to BNC outputs so an oscilloscope can be connected. The processor inputs are each connected to a variable voltage divider and to BNC connectors so the inputs can be examined on an oscilloscope. The circuit can be operated in two modes: the pulsing mode

4049

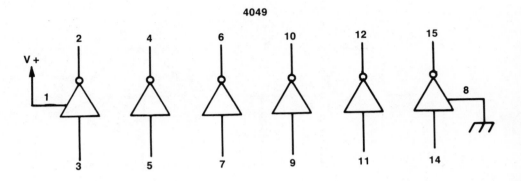

4066

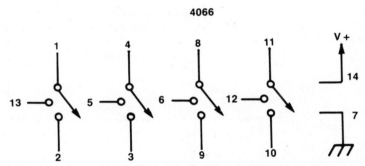

Fig. 4-8. Pinout diagram of CMOS 4049 and 4066 chips.

allows oscilloscope examination of the inputs and the outputs; the dc mode allows LED observation of the output. The pulsing circuit is two 4049 CMOS inverters wired to give a clock signal or square wave (Mims, 1982).

In the dc mode, start with a condition such that both LED's are lit. This is equivalent to a (0,0) input, since we are using inverters, a low input gives a high output. Adjusting potentiometer B, so LED B just turns off is equivalent to biasing the input to processor B, until it is a high logic. A high input results in a low output and the LED turns off. By adjusting potentiometer A so it is biased to a point where LED A turns off, causes the summed inputs at processor B to go low, and LED B goes high and turns on. By very careful adjustment of the potentiometers it is possible to observe the system flip back between A and B while increasing the bias on each processor. Oscilloscope measurements indicate that the threshold input is about 2.5V. When the sum of the inputs is greater than 2.5V the output will be a low logic. You can see that CMOS inverters have a transfer curve like one that was shown in Fig. 4-1.

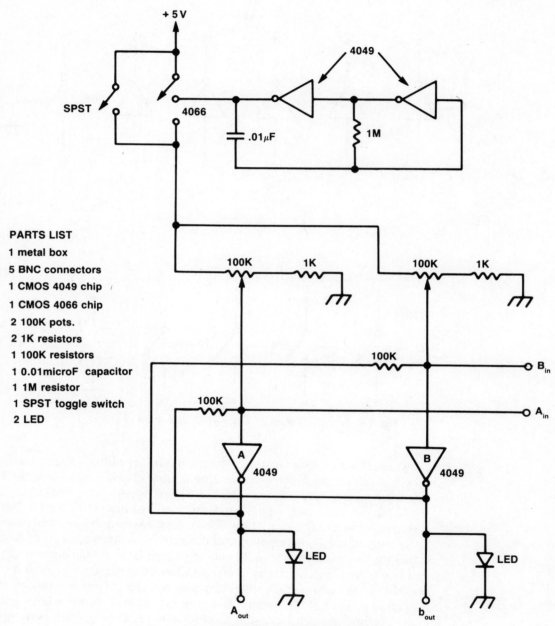

PARTS LIST

1 metal box

5 BNC connectors

1 CMOS 4049 chip

1 CMOS 4066 chip

2 100K pots.

2 1K resistors

1 100K resistors

1 0.01microF capacitor

1 1M resistor

1 SPST toggle switch

2 LED

Fig. 4-9. Adjustable biased flip-flop.

Photo 4-1. Artificial neural flip-flop circuit.

PROJECT 2: AN INTERFACEABLE N-FLOP CIRCUIT ─────────

The next circuit discussed is the N-flop. The simple two-processor flip-flop could be used to compute which line has a greater input signal. If the input state is (0,1), then the output state is (1,0). This idea of using the two-processor circuit to calculate which bit is high can be extended to an N-flop circuit. The N-flop consists of N processors, each connected to every other one with an inhibitory connection. Each resistor connection has the same value (100K). Taking an example to see what the N-flop does, run program NEURON4P, from Chapter 3.

For an eight-processor circuit the connection matrix would be

$$
T = \begin{bmatrix}
0 & 1 & 1 & 1 & 1 & 1 & 1 & 1 \\
1 & 0 & 1 & 1 & 1 & 1 & 1 & 1 \\
1 & 1 & 0 & 1 & 1 & 1 & 1 & 1 \\
1 & 1 & 1 & 0 & 1 & 1 & 1 & 1 \\
1 & 1 & 1 & 1 & 0 & 1 & 1 & 1 \\
1 & 1 & 1 & 1 & 1 & 0 & 1 & 1 \\
1 & 1 & 1 & 1 & 1 & 1 & 0 & 1 \\
1 & 1 & 1 & 1 & 1 & 1 & 1 & 0
\end{bmatrix}
$$

In this simulation run, enter anything for the seed value. For threshold, enter 0. Answer the question for operator entered input vector, as 1, for yes. Also answer the question for operator entered T matrix as 1 for yes.

Enter the T matrix just shown, and enter an eight-bit vector with only one bit high and the other seven bits low. Figure 4-10 shows the results for four input vectors and their computed output vector. Notice all bits have flipped. The N-flop could be used to check for one high bit in a vector. The next circuit to be discussed is another type of flip-flop circuit.

The flip-flop circuit to be described was interfaced to an AT&T 6300 computer (IBM clone). The circuit itself consists of four interpenetrating, two-neuron flip-flops, for a total of eight neurons. We will first look at the interface circuit and then the electronic neural network circuit. A block diagram of the overall circuit is given in Fig. 4-11.

The interface board can be made by the experimenter using an Intel 8255 programmable peripheral interface chip (Goldsbrough, 1979). It is more convenient, however, to use an off-the-shelf board. Qua Tech, in Akron, Ohio, offers an interface board that works very well. The PXB-721 board from Qua Tech consists of three 8255 PPI chips. Each chip has three 8-bit ports that can be software configured to act as input or output ports. This gives a total of 72 lines for input/output experimentation. The PXB-721 board contains three headers, each consists of the 24 I/O lines, logic control, and power lines. The

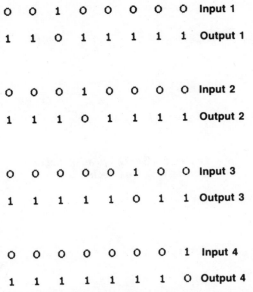

Fig. 4-10. Computer simulation results of small N-flop circuit. Seed 0, Info. 0, Threshold 0.

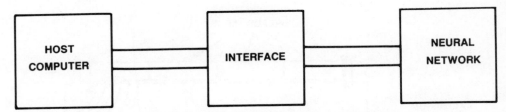

Fig. 4-11. Block diagram of interface experiment.

Qua Tech design allows cables to be connected to the headers and then plugged into other Qua Tech boards for data acquisition and control. By modification of the cables it is possible to bring the 72 I/O lines outside the computer and solder them to an experimenter breadboard.

The pin out diagram of the PXB-721 board is given in Fig. 4-12. After building extension cables that come out of the back of the computer, solder the cable ends to the bottom side of an experimenter breadboard, such as Radio Shack #276-174. Because there are 72 I/O lines you will need at least one of the RS #276-174 breadboards. Attaching a few more experimenter breadboards to the system allows ample space to build circuits that will be interfaced to the computer via the I/O lines. Figure 4-13 is an overall sketch of the interfaced experimenter breadboard.

PA0	1	18	PA1
PA2	2	19	PA3
PA4	3	20	PA5
PA6	4	21	PA7
GND	5	22	GND
+5V	6	23	+5V
+12V	7	24	+12V
PC0	8	25	PC1
PC2	9	26	PC3
PC4	10	27	PC5
PC6	11	28	PC7
−12V	12	29	−5V
RST	13	30	GND
PB0	14	31	PB1
PB2	15	32	PB3
PB4	16	33	PB5
PB6	17	34	PB7

*Fig. 4-12. PXB-721 header diagram
(courtesy of Qua Tech).*

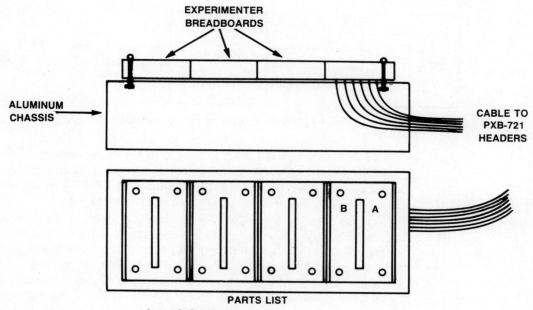

PARTS LIST
1 metal chassis (9 × 7)
4 experimenter sockets Radio Shack #276-174
4ft. ribbon cable

Fig. 4-13. Sketch of experimenter breadboard.

It is convenient to "unscramble" the wires from the cables and put them in an order that is easy to remember on the breadboard. Table 4-1 shows a suggested arrangement for the wiring.

Table 4-1. Pinouts on the Protoboard and Their Function.

Protoboard pin	8255 function	Protoboard pin	8255 function
A1	PA0	A19	PC2
A2	PA1	A20	PC3
A3	PA2	A21	PC4
A4	PA3	A22	PC5
A5	PA4	A23	PC6
A6	PA5	A24	PC7
A7	PA6	A25	PA0
A8	PA7	A26	PA1
A9	PB0	A27	PA2
A10	PB1	A28	PA3
A11	PB2	A29	PA4
A12	PB3	A30	PA5
A13	PB4	A31	PA6
A14	PB5	A32	PA7
A15	PB6	A33	PB0
A16	PB7	A34	PB1
A17	PC0	A35	PB2
A18	PC1	A36	PB3

Protoboard pin	8255 function	Protoboard pin	8255 function
B1	PB4	B19	PA6
B2	PB5	B20	PA7
B3	PB6	B21	PB0
B4	PB7	B22	PB1
B5	PC0	B23	PB2
B6	PC1	B24	PB3
B7	PC2	B25	PB4
B8	PC3	B26	PB5
B9	PC4	B27	PB6
B10	PC5	B28	PB7
B11	PC6	B29	PC0
B12	PC7	B30	PC1
B13	PA0	B31	PC2
B14	PA1	B32	PC3
B15	PA2	B33	PC4
B16	PA3	B34	PC5
B17	PA4	B35	PC6
B18	PA5	B36	PC7

Let's discuss communication with the interface breadboard. The 72 I/O lines on the experimenter board can be addressed from software. The control words for each port of each header are given in Table 4-2.

Table 4-2. Port Configuration of the Interface Board.

Header 1	
I/O Location	Port
XX0H	A
XX1H	B
XX2H	C
XX3H	Control

Header 2	
I/O Location	Port
XX4H	A
XX5H	B
XX6H	C
XX7H	Control

Header 3	
I/O Location	Port
XX8H	A
XX9H	B
XXAH	C
XXBH	Control

The number XX is set by the 10 switches on the PXB-721 board. The board is shipped with address 30BH. The board must be used in mode 0. This is the basic input/output mode. Modes 1 and 2 are for other Qua Tech modules. Table 4-3 shows the control word and port configuration. Further details on programming the Qua Tech PBX-721 board can be found in the product's technical operating manual.

Let's examine the electronic neural network circuit and the program to communicate with it through the interface breadboard. As pointed out earlier, this neural network circuit consists of four interpenetrating neural flip-flops. In this circuit all the allowed states will have equal energy. The connection matrix is

$$T = \begin{bmatrix} 0 & 0 & 0 & 0 & 0 & 0 & 0 & 1 \\ 0 & 0 & 0 & 0 & 0 & 0 & 1 & 0 \\ 0 & 0 & 0 & 0 & 0 & 1 & 0 & 0 \\ 0 & 0 & 0 & 0 & 1 & 0 & 0 & 0 \\ 0 & 0 & 0 & 1 & 0 & 0 & 0 & 0 \\ 0 & 0 & 1 & 0 & 0 & 0 & 0 & 0 \\ 0 & 1 & 0 & 0 & 0 & 0 & 0 & 0 \\ 1 & 0 & 0 & 0 & 0 & 0 & 0 & 0 \end{bmatrix}$$

Table 4-3. Qua Tech Module Control Word and Port Configuration.

Control	Port A	Port B	Port C	
CONTENT	PA7-PA0	PB7-PB0	PC7-PC4	PC3-PC0
80H	OUTPUT	OUTPUT	OUTPUT	OUTPUT
81H	OUTPUT	OUTPUT	OUTPUT	INPUT
82H	OUTPUT	INPUT	OUTPUT	OUTPUT
83H	OUTPUT	INPUT	OUTPUT	INPUT
88H	OUTPUT	OUTPUT	INPUT	OUTPUT
89H	OUTPUT	OUTPUT	INPUT	INPUT
8AH	OUTPUT	INPUT	INPUT	OUTPUT
8BH	OUTPUT	INPUT	INPUT	INPUT
90H	INPUT	OUTPUT	OUTPUT	OUTPUT
91H	INPUT	OUTPUT	OUTPUT	INPUT
92H	INPUT	INPUT	OUTPUT	OUTPUT
93H	INPUT	INPUT	OUTPUT	INPUT
98H	INPUT	OUTPUT	INPUT	OUTPUT
99H	INPUT	OUTPUT	INPUT	INPUT
9AH	INPUT	INPUT	INPUT	OUTPUT
9BH	INPUT	INPUT	INPUT	INPUT

The threshold logic processors are the CMOS inverter gates operating in the linear regime. Each processor is connected to the other according to the connection matrix T. From this matrix we see that neuron #1 is connected to neuron #8 and that neuron #8 is connected to neuron #1. This is obvious, because the matrix elements T18 and T81 have a value of 1. Summarizing the matrix: Neuron #2 is connected to neuron #7 and neuron #7 is connected to neuron #2. Neuron #3 is connected to neuron #6 and neuron #6 is connected to neuron #3. Neuron #4 is connected to neuron #5 and neuron #5 is connected to neuron #4. The +1 in the matrix represents inhibiting connections and the 0 represents no connection. The inhibiting connection is a 100K resistor in the appropriate place. It was shown in Chapters 2 and 3 that a two-state neuron and a binary matrix represents a good model of neural networks. It differs from those models that use excitatory connections by a shift in the operating conditions.

The circuit is shown in Fig. 4-14 and the pin out diagrams are given in Fig. 4-15.

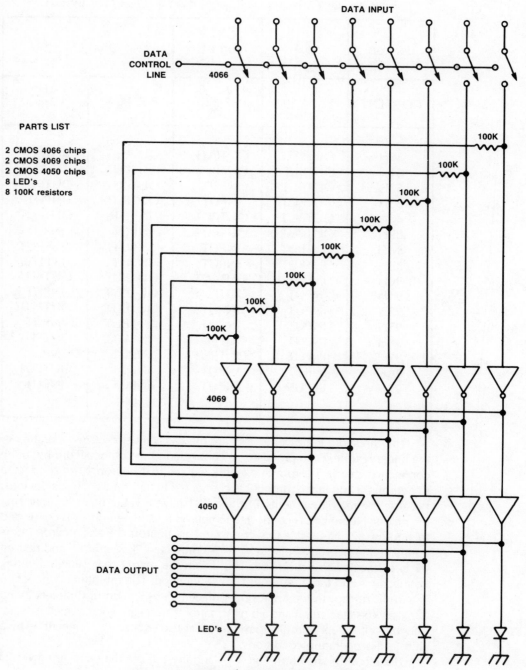

Fig. 4-14. Schematic for flip-flop experiment.

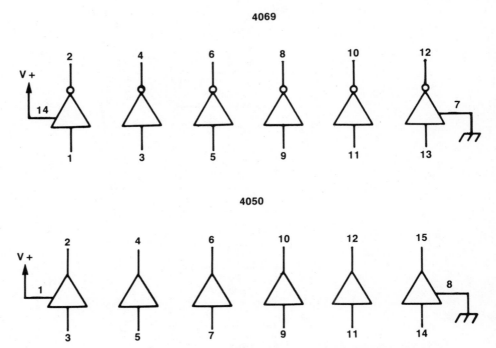

Fig. 4-15. Pinout diagram of CMOS 4069 and 4050 chips.

From Fig. 4-15, it can be seen that the row of neurons are the CMOS 4069 inverters. In the circuit the 4069's were used because they more closely represent the ideal transfer function represented in Fig. 4-1. The row of CMOS 4050 buffers are used as high impedance buffers to drive the LED's, and to provide a signal for the computer input lines. The connection matrix is clearly seen. It is represented by the matrix of 100K resistors. The data output from the computer is input to the electronic neural network by the CMOS 4066 analog switches. All these switches are operated by one control line from the computer.

To use the network, an 8-bit vector is presented to the 4066 switches. The switches are then closed for a moment to "charge" the network. The switches are then opened again by the control line, and the network is allowed to run free in order to compute the stable state. This computation consists of the electronic signal going around and around many times in one second until the final stable state is displayed as an 8-bit vector at the LED's. After the network settles, the data lines are read, and the *answer* is displayed on the CRT of the computer. The iterated calculations of the network models in Chapter 3 are similar to these electronic circuits.

We will next examine the program NETWORKP and a RUN of the program. A flow chart is shown in Fig. 4-16. From the flow chart it appears that there

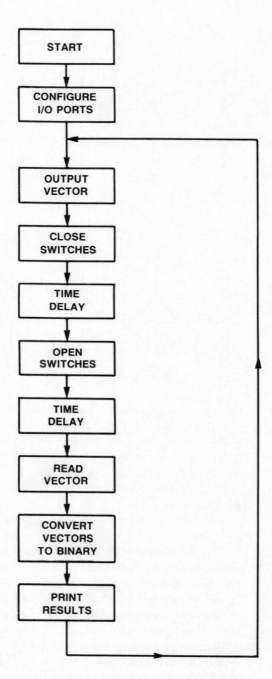

Fig. 4-16. Simplified program flow chart for interface experiment.

is no END. Actually the program ends after all 256 possible 8-bit vectors have been tested by the network. Line 10 sets the dimensions for two small arrays to hold binary vectors. Lines 20-50 are for configuration of the Qua Tech board. The program starts in the J loop at line 60. The J value is the decimal equivalent of the 8-bit binary vector presented to the network in line 70. The CMOS 4066 switches are closed by line 80, and are held closed while the network charges for a count of 1000 in line 90. The switches are opened up in line 100, and the network is allowed to settle in line 110. The network is read by the computer in line 120. After some name changes in lines 130-140, then the vector read from the network is converted from decimal to binary in lines 150-310, and stored in the A array in line 320. The decimal vector sent to the network is converted to binary in lines 330-490, and stored in the B array in line 500. The vector sent to the network is printed in decimal and binary, followed by the vector read from the network. These printed vectors are sent to the line printer.

```
NETWORKP

 10 DIM A(10),B(10)
 20 OUT &H303,&H80 'PORT 1A AND 1B AS OUTPUT PORTS
 30 OUT &H307,&H92 'PORT 2A AND 2B AS INPUT PORTS
 40 OUT 0B,&H80 'PORT 3A AS OUTPUT PORT FOR CONTROL PURPOSES
 50 OUT &H300,&H0 'OUTPUT 0 ON PORT 1A
 60 FOR J=0 TO 255
 70 OUT &H300,J
 80 OUT &H301,1
 90 FOR I=1 TO 1000 : NEXT I
100 OUT &H301,0
110 FOR I=1 TO 1000 : NEXT I
120 A=INP(&H304) 'INPUT FROM PORT 2A
130 Y=J : REM Y = OUTPUT
135 B=J
140 X=A : REM X = INPUT
150 A1=0:A2=0:A3=0:A4=0:A5=0:A6=0:A7=0:A8=0
160 IF A-2^7<0 THEN GOTO 180
170 A=A-2^7:AB=1
180 IF A-2^6<0 THEN GOTO 200
190 A=A-2^6:A7=1
200 IF A-2^5<0 THEN GOTO 220
210 A=A-2^5:A6=1
220 IF A-2^4<0 THEN GOTO 240
230 A=A-2^4:A5=1
240 IF A-2^3<0 THEN GOTO 260
250 A=A-2^3:A4=1
```

```
260 IF A-2^2<0 THEN GOTO 280
270 A=A-2^2:A3=1
280 IF A-2^1<0 THEN GOTO 300
290 A=A-2^1:A2=1
300 IF A-2^0<0 THEN GOTO 320
310 A=A-2^0:A1=1
320   A(8)=A8:A(7)=A7:A(6)=A6:A(5)=A5:A(4)=A4:A(3)=A3
:A(2)=A2:A(1)=A1
330 B8=0:B7=0:B6=0:B5=0:B4=0:B3=0:B2=0:B1=0
340 IF B-2^7<0 THEN GOTO 360
350 B=B-2^7:B8=1
360 IF B-2^6<0 THEN GOTO 380
370 B=B-2^6:B7=1
380 IF B-2^5<0 THEN GOTO 400
390 B=B-2^5:B6=1
400 IF B-2^4<0 THEN GOTO 420
410 B=B-2^4:B5=1
420 IF B-2^3<0 THEN GOTO 440
430 B=B-2^3:B4=1
440 IF B-2^2<0 THEN GOTO 460
450 B=B-2^2:B3=1
460 IF B-2^1<0 THEN GOTO 480
470 B=B-2^1:B2=1
480 IF B-2^0<0 THEN GOTO 500
490 B=B-2^0:B1=1
500   B(8)=B8:B(7)=B7:B(6)=B6:B(5)=B5:B(4)=B4:B(3)=B3
:B(2)=B2:B(1)=B1
510 LPRINT Y,"   ";
520 FOR K=8 TO STEP -1
530 LPRINT B(K);
540 NEXT K
550 LPRINT
560 LPRINT X,"   ";
570 FOR K=8 TO 1 STEP -1
580 LPRINT A(K);
590 NEXT K
600 LPRINT
610 LPRINT
620 LPRINT
630 NEXT J
```

The output from a RUN of this program isn't hard to understand. If we present the vector (0 0 0 0 0 0 0 1) to the network, the computed vector must be of the form, (1 X X X X X 0). Because neuron #1 is connected to neuron #8 and neuron #8 is connected to neuron #1, then bit 0 and bit 7 must flip. The other six bits will settle to whatever state they can, based on component noise and component variations. Table 4-4 shows all the stable states computed for this circuit. Because this circuit has 8 neurons there are 2^8 stable states.

Table 4-4. Stable States Computed for Fig. 4-14.

1 1 1 1 0 0 0 0	0 1 1 0 1 0 0 1
0 0 0 0 1 1 1 1	1 0 0 1 0 1 1 0
0 1 1 1 0 0 0 1	1 0 1 0 1 0 1 0
1 0 1 1 0 0 1 0	1 1 0 0 1 1 0 0
1 1 0 1 0 1 0 0	1 0 0 0 1 1 1 0
1 1 1 0 1 0 0 0	0 1 0 0 1 1 0 1
0 0 1 1 0 0 1 1	0 0 1 0 1 0 1 1
0 1 0 1 0 1 0 1	0 0 0 1 0 1 1 1

Recall that given an N-neuron circuit, the state space is an N-dimensional hypercube, and all the corners (2^N) of this hypercube are stable states. Since only 16 stable states were computed, the other stable states must be metastable states and not have the energy depth of the 16 computed states. Appendix A is a complete computer print out from the above experiment.

At this point, an interesting experiment might be to build an 8-flop circuit on the breadboard and experiment with it.

CONTENT-ADDRESSABLE MEMORY CIRCUITS

The content-addressable memory circuit discussed in Chapter 2 can be modeled in electronic hardware. The problem with these circuits is that for N neurons there are N^2 synapse resistors, which means $2N^2$ wires. The next circuit is a small programmable electronic neural network. By programmable, I mean the synapse resistors are easily changed by the user. Using the program NEURON8P, it is possible to generate a matrix and then plug resistors in the appropriate place in the synapse matrix to complete the hardware programming. An input vector can be loaded from the front panel by toggle switches. By letting the network run free, it will compute the best stable state and display the answer on LED's or a computer interface.

PROJECT 3: ELECTRONIC NEURAL COMPUTER

Figure 4-17 is a schematic diagram and Photo 4-2 is the picture of the completed electronic neural computer.

As can be seen from Fig. 4-17, this electronic neural computer contains eight neurons. As in previous circuits, CMOS 4069 inverters are used as the threshold logic processors, CMOS 4050 buffers as drivers, and CMOS 4066 switches to isolate the network and let it "float" or "run-free" during the computation stage of operation. The rows of IC sockets allow easy plug in of resistors. The resistor is plugged into the appropriate row-column position from the T matrix. Photo 4-2 also shows screw terminals for +5V power connection, and a DIP header cable for output to a digital computer. This cable could be plugged into the interface described earlier in this chapter.

The network is easy to use. After selecting which matrix elements will receive a resistor, plug 100K resistors in the IC socket at the appropriate T_{ij} position. Then connect the network to a +5V power supply. Flip the load/run switch to the load position and load the input vector from the row of toggle switches. The LED's will indicate the input vector at this stage. Note, we are using reverse logic, therefore logic 1 will be a turned off LED and a logic 0 will be a turned on LED. After the vector is loaded, flip the load/run switch to the run position. This cuts the input to the amplifiers. The network will settle down in a few milliseconds, and the computed answer will be displayed as a vector on the LED's, again in reverse logic.

Let's use the network in an experiment and see how well it performs in content-addressing. The results of this experiment will be compared with a digital computer simulation from the program NEURON8P.

Figure 4-18 shows a run of NEURON8P. The actual seed, threshold, and info values are not important. The T matrix is symmetric. Note that row 4 and row 7, as well as column 4 and 7 are empty. This means there are no connections to processors 4 and 7. These floating processors are significant, as will be seen later in this chapter. Notice from Fig. 4-18, the first vector leads to a two cycle, the second vector to a stable state, the third vector to the same state, and the fourth vector leads to the same two cycle. The other input vectors lead to the same stable state obtained earlier. Now, plugging the 100K resistors in place in the electronic neural computer and loading the vector (1 1 1 1 1 1 1 1), you get a computed vector (1 0 1 1 0 0 1 1). This vector is the complement of the vector (0 1 0 0 1 1 0 0), which is one of the cycle points in the two cycle from the digital simulation. But, the circuit does not oscillate between the two states. You see this is a stable state. If you now load the stable state vector (0 1 0 0 1 1 0 0) and flip to run mode, you see this is a stable state only for a moment. What happened? Why did these two LED's go to logic 1? What happens if you load this vector now? Loading the vector (0 1 0 1 1 1 1 0), you see that it is a stable state. Just what is going on here?

The LED's #4 and #7 float from logic 0 to logic 1 because there are no connections to processors #4 and #7. This is equivalent to having a small antenna hooked up to these processors. They pick up enough static charge to float to a high logic.

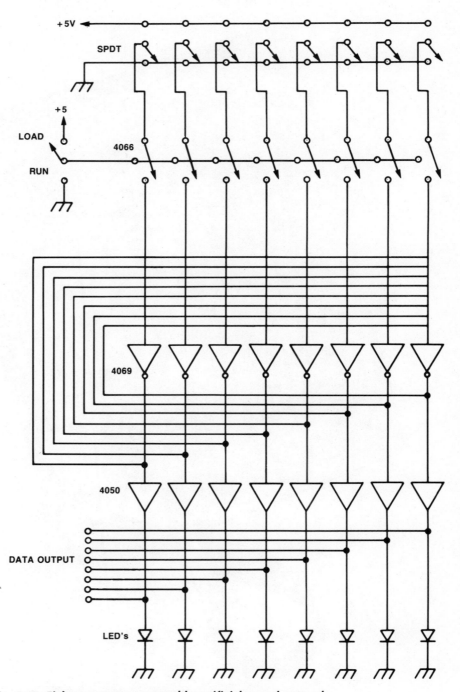

PARTS LIST

1 hedder cable
9 SPDT toggle switches
2 screw terminals
4 14 pin sockets
43 16 pin sockets
8 LED's
2 CMOS 4069 chips
2 CMOS 4066 chips
2 CMOS 4050 chips
1 metal chassis (9 × 7)
1 Vector board (9 × 7)

Fig. 4-17. Eight-neuron programmable artificial neural network.

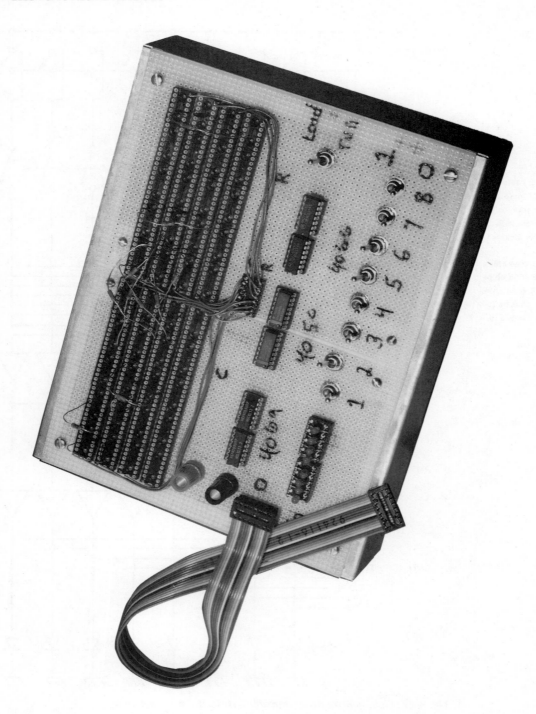

Photo 4-2. Small neural computer.

MATRIX

```
O  1  O  O  O  1  O  O
1  O  1  O  O  O  O  O
O  1  O  O  1  1  O  O
O  O  O  O  O  O  O  O
O  O  1  O  O  O  O  1
1  O  1  O  O  O  O  O
O  O  O  O  O  O  O  O
O  O  O  O  1  O  O  O
```

Input 1	O	O	O	O	O	1	O	O	Input 9	O	O	O	O	1	O	O	1
Output 1	1	O	1	O	O	O	O	O	Output 9	O	O	1	O	1	O	O	1
			ENERGY	O								ENERGY	−1				
Input 2	1	O	1	O	O	O	O	O	Input 10	O	O	1	O	1	O	O	1
Output 2	O	1	O	O	1	1	O	O	Output 10	O	1	1	O	1	1	O	1
			ENERGY	O								ENERGY	−1.5				
Input 3	O	1	O	O	1	1	O	O	Input 11	O	1	1	O	1	1	O	1
Output 3	1	O	1	O	O	O	O	1	Output 11	1	1	1	O	1	1	O	1
			ENERGY	O								ENERGY	−2.5				
Input 4	1	O	1	O	O	O	O	1	Input 12	1	1	1	O	1	1	O	1
Output 4	O	1	O	O	1	1	O	O	Output 12	1	1	1	O	1	1	O	1
			ENERGY	O								ENERGY	−3				
Input 5	O	1	O	O	1	1	O	O	Input 13	1	1	1	O	1	1	O	1
Output 5	1	O	1	O	O	O	O	1	Output 13	1	1	1	O	1	1	O	1
			ENERGY	O								ENERGY	−3				
Input 6	1	O	1	O	O	O	O	1	Input 14	1	1	1	O	1	1	O	1
Output 6	O	1	O	O	1	1	O	O	Output 14	1	1	1	O	1	1	O	1
			ENERGY	O								ENERGY	−3				
Input 7	O	1	O	O	1	1	O	O	Input 15	1	1	1	O	1	1	O	1
Output 7	1	O	1	O	O	O	O	1	Output 15	1	1	1	O	1	1	O	1
			ENERGY	O								ENERGY	−3				
Input 8	1	O	1	O	O	O	O	1	Input 16	1	1	1	O	1	1	O	1
Output 8	O	1	O	O	1	1	O	O	Output 16	1	1	1	O	1	1	O	1
			ENERGY	O								ENERGY	−3				

Fig. 4-18. Example run of program NEURON8P.

```
Input 17   O  1  O  1  1  1  1  1        Input 33   1  O  1  O  O  O  1  O
Output 17  1  O  1  O  1  O  O  1        Output 33  O  1  O  O  1  1  O  O
           ENERGY  -1                              ENERGY  O
Input 18   1  O  1  O  1  O  O  1        Input 34   O  1  O  O  1  1  O  O
Output 18  O  1  1  O  1  1  O  1        Output 34  1  O  1  O  O  O  O  1
           ENERGY  -1.5                            ENERGY  O
Input 19   O  1  1  O  1  1  O  1        Input 35   1  O  1  O  O  O  O  1
Output 19  1  1  1  O  1  1  O  1        Output 35  O  1  O  O  1  1  O  O
           ENERGY  -2.5                            ENERGY  O
Input 20   1  1  1  O  1  1  O  1        Input 36   O  1  O  O  1  1  O  O
Output 20  1  1  1  O  1  1  O  1        Output 36  1  O  1  O  O  O  O  1
           ENERGY  -3                              ENERGY  O
Input 21   1  1  1  O  1  1  O  1        Input 37   1  O  1  O  O  O  O  1
Output 21  1  1  1  O  1  1  O  1        Output 37  O  1  O  O  1  1  O  O
           ENERGY  -3                              ENERGY  O
Input 22   1  1  1  O  1  1  O  1        Input 38   O  1  O  O  1  1  O  O
Output 22  1  1  1  O  1  1  O  1        Output 38  1  O  1  O  O  O  O  1
           ENERGY  -3                              ENERGY  O
Input 23   1  1  1  O  1  1  O  1        Input 39   1  O  1  O  O  O  O  1
Output 23  1  1  1  O  1  1  O  1        Output 39  O  1  O  O  1  1  O  O
           ENERGY  -3                              ENERGY  O
Input 24   1  1  1  O  1  1  O  1        Input 40   O  1  O  O  1  1  O  O
Output 24  1  1  1  O  1  1  O  1        Output 40  1  O  1  O  O  O  O  1
           ENERGY  -3                              ENERGY  O
Input 25   O  O  O  O  1  1  1  O        Input 41   O  O  1  O  1  O  O  O
Output 25  1  O  1  O  O  O  O  1        Output 41  O  1  1  O  1  1  O  1
           ENERGY  O                               ENERGY  -1
Input 26   1  O  1  O  O  O  O  1        Input 42   O  1  1  O  1  1  O  1
Output 26  O  1  O  O  1  1  O  O        Output 42  1  1  1  O  1  1  O  1
           ENERGY  O                               ENERGY  -2.5
Input 27   O  1  O  O  1  1  O  O        Input 43   1  1  1  O  1  1  O  1
Output 27  1  O  1  O  O  O  O  1        Output 43  1  1  1  O  1  1  O  1
           ENERGY  O                               ENERGY  -3
Input 28   1  O  1  O  O  O  O  1        Input 44   1  1  1  O  1  1  O  1
Output 28  O  1  O  O  1  1  O  O        Output 44  1  1  1  O  1  1  O  1
           ENERGY  O                               ENERGY  -3
Input 29   O  1  O  O  1  1  O  O        Input 45   1  1  1  O  1  1  O  1
Output 29  1  O  1  O  O  O  O  1        Output 45  1  1  1  O  1  1  O  1
           ENERGY  O                               ENERGY  -3
Input 30   1  O  1  O  O  O  O  1        Input 46   1  1  1  O  1  1  O  1
Output 30  O  1  O  O  1  1  O  O        Output 46  1  1  1  O  1  1  O  1
           ENERGY  O                               ENERGY  -3
Input 31   O  1  O  O  1  1  O  O        Input 47   1  1  1  O  1  1  O  1
Output 31  1  O  1  O  O  O  O  1        Output 47  1  1  1  O  1  1  O  1
           ENERGY  O                               ENERGY  -3
Input 32   1  O  1  O  O  O  O  1        Input 48   1  1  1  O  1  1  O  1
Output 32  O  1  O  O  1  1  O  O        Output 48  1  1  1  O  1  1  O  1
           ENERGY  O                               ENERGY  -3
```

Input 49	1	O	O	O	1	O	1	O
Output 49	O	1	1	O	O	1	O	1
			ENERGY	O				
Input 50	O	1	1	O	O	1	O	1
Output 50	1	1	1	O	1	1	O	O
			ENERGY	-1.5				
Input 51	1	1	1	O	1	1	O	O
Output 51	1	1	1	O	1	1	O	1
			ENERGY	-2.5				
Input 52	1	1	1	O	1	1	O	1
Output 52	1	1	1	O	1	1	O	1
			ENERGY	-3				
Input 53	1	1	1	O	1	1	O	1
Output 53	1	1	1	O	1	1	O	1
			ENERGY	-3				
Input 54	1	1	1	O	1	1	O	1
Output 54	1	1	1	O	1	1	O	1
			ENERGY	-3				
Input 55	1	1	1	O	1	1	O	1
Output 55	1	1	1	O	1	1	O	1
			ENERGY	-3				
Input 56	1	1	1	O	1	1	O	1
Output 56	1	1	1	O	1	1	O	1
			ENERGY	-3				

Input 57	O	O	1	O	1	O	O	1
Output 57	O	1	1	O	1	1	O	1
			ENERGY	-1.5				
Input 58	O	1	1	O	1	1	O	1
Output 58	1	1	1	O	1	1	O	1
			ENERGY	-2.5				
Input 59	1	1	1	O	1	1	O	1
Output 59	1	1	1	O	1	1	O	1
			ENERGY	-3				
Input 60	1	1	1	O	1	1	O	1
Output 60	1	1	1	O	1	1	O	1
			ENERGY	-3				
Input 61	1	1	1	O	1	1	O	1
Output 61	1	1	1	O	1	1	O	1
			ENERGY	-3				
Input 62	1	1	1	O	1	1	O	1
Output 62	1	1	1	O	1	1	O	1
			ENERGY	-3				
Input 63	1	1	1	O	1	1	O	1
Output 63	1	1	1	O	1	1	O	1
			ENERGY	-3				
Input 64	1	1	1	O	1	1	O	1
Output 64	1	1	1	O	1	1	O	1
			ENERGY	-3				

There are more digital computed stable states, including a two cycle, than there are ones computed by the electronic neural computer. As pointed out in Chapter 3, electronic component noise will cause the network to settle to the most stable state. The digital computer simulations include metastable states. Reiterating, given an N-neuron circuit, then all the corners of an N-dimensional hypercube (2^N) are stable or metastable states.

Use the associative learning rule in program HEBB3P to generate a matrix and compare the simulated results with those from the neural computer. Figure 4-19 is a run of the program HEBB3P, using one memory state. The memory vector to generate the matrix was (0 1 0 0 0 1 0 0). Placing the 100K resistors in the electronic neural computer and operating, we see that this vector is a metastable state. From the digital simulation we see that the vector (0 0 0 0 0 1 0 0) is a metastable state. In the electronic network, when the vector (0 1 0 0 0 1 0 0) is loaded and left in the run position, the network will drift to the state (0 0 0 0 0 1 0 0) indicating that this vector is most stable in the electronic neural network. This drifting off to another state is probably caused by electronic noise. In this case, processor #2 is connected and should not act as an antenna to pick up a static charge.

MATRIX

```
0  0  0  0  0  0  0  0
0  0  0  0  0  1  0  0
0  0  0  0  0  0  0  0
0  0  0  0  0  0  0  0
0  0  0  0  0  0  0  0
0  1  0  0  0  0  0  0
0  0  0  0  0  0  0  0
0  0  0  0  0  0  0  0
```

Input 1	1	1	0	0	0	1	0	1	**Input 6**	0	0	0	0	1	1	0	0
Output 1	0	1	0	0	0	1	0	0	**Output 6**	0	0	0	0	0	1	0	0
Input 2	1	1	1	1	1	0	1	0	**Input 7**	0	0	0	1	1	1	1	1
Output 2	0	1	0	0	0	0	0	0	**Output 7**	0	0	0	0	0	1	0	0
Input 3	0	1	0	0	1	1	0	1	**Input 8**	0	1	1	1	0	0	1	0
Output 3	0	1	0	0	0	1	0	0	**Output 8**	0	1	0	0	0	0	0	0
Input 4	1	0	0	0	0	1	1	0	**Input 9**	0	0	0	1	0	1	1	0
Output 4	0	0	0	0	0	1	0	0	**Output 9**	0	0	0	0	0	1	0	0
Input 5	1	0	0	0	1	0	1	1									
Output 5	0	0	0	0	0	0	0	0									

Fig. 4-19. Example run of program HEBB3P.

ADVANCED EXPERIMENT SUGGESTIONS

More advanced circuit ideas for the ambitious experimenter will be examined in this section. Obviously the next level of experiments would be to build a larger electronic neural network. It has been said that, studying the behavior of small electronic neural networks with only a few neurons is like studying grid lock with only a few cars. It can be speculated that the spurious states sometimes produced is analogous to creative activity in humans. In humans, two ideas overlap and generate a new idea. In electronic neural networks, two vectors can overlap in Hamming space. When too many processors are too densely connected the overlapping vectors produce spurious states. Is this creativity by collective networks?

The problem with large networks is that for N processors we need N^2 connections. This can be a lot of wiring. Programmability is another problem. An obvious solution is to wire all the resistors in place in the network with a 4066 switch in series. Then a control code can address each switch, to connect or disconnect the resistor from the matrix. To minimize the number of wires, you could use a serial-in parallel-out shift register. The programmable network could also be implemented with CdS photocells as synapse connections. A light beam could then activate the appropriate cells. This might be a type of hybrid optical-neural computer.

Another idea is to build a layered network. One network receives an input vector from sensors or switches. The output from this network is then fed as the input to another network. This idea was suggested in Fig. 2-5. The behavior of this system could be very interesting.

The last project suggestion is an electronic neural network with inhibitory and excitatory connections. Figure 4-20 shows a schematic for a three-neuron circuit. The circuit includes excitatory and inhibitory connections at the crosspoints. For this type circuit the T matrix contains $+1$ and -1 values, as well as 0 values. The basic circuit model is given by the equation:

$$
V_i = \begin{cases} -1 \text{ if } \sum_j T_{ij} V_j < 0 \\ +1 \text{ if } \sum_j T_{ij} V_j \geq 0 \end{cases}
$$

The next chapter discusses the future of neural computing.

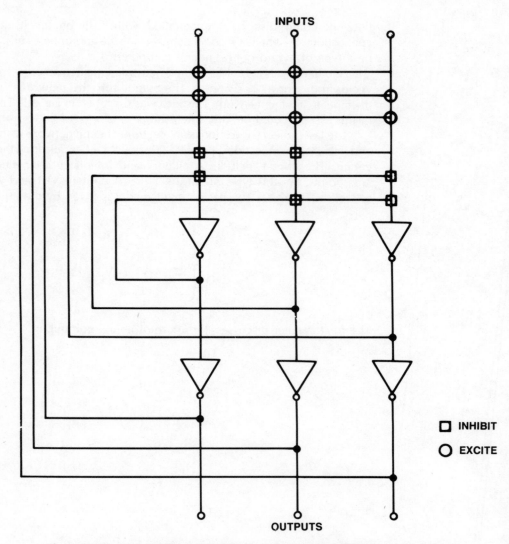

Fig. 4-20. Simple neural circuit with excitatory and inhibitory connections.

5

Neural
Computing

This chapter introduces neural networks from a biological viewpoint. Following the biological networks I will introduce other learning rules and neural network refinements. In the next section I will discuss VLSI (Very Large Scale Integration) neural networks and applications of neural computing. In the final section I will speculate on the future technologies and list corporations involved in neural networking.

BIOLOGICAL MODELS

Biologists use neural circuit models to understand behavior. Two such models I will discuss here are a pattern generator, and a learning mechanism.

In real organic neurons, the firing of the neuron is a burst of pulses at a certain frequency. The input level reaches a threshold value and the neuron fires a fast burst of pulses similar to that shown in Fig. 5-1.

In Fig. 5-1 the neuron has fired two bursts of pulses. These pulse bursts can be observed with micro-electrodes implanted in the neurons. Getting (1985) has used this technique to map out the swimming behavior of the sea slug, Tritonia diomedea. Swimming behavior, like walking, involves a set of neurons or a circuit called a central pattern generator. A simplified circuit diagram of the central pattern generator is shown in Fig. 5-2.

The circuit element, DSI, is a few neurons connected to dorsal swimming muscle fibers. The VSI element is connected to ventral swimming muscle fibers. And the element C2 is an interneuron simply called cerebral cell 2. The connections in the circuit diagram marked I are inhibitory and E is excitatory connections. When DSI depolarizes it begins to fire. This depolarization can be caused by the escape response initiated by contact with

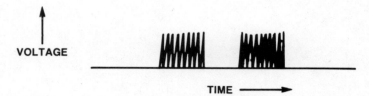

VOLTAGE

TIME ——→

Fig. 5-1. Sketch of pulse burst for real organic neuron. Two pulse bursts shown.

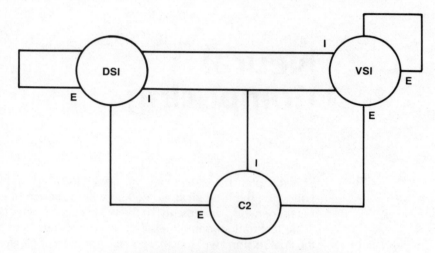

Fig. 5-2. Simplified circuit diagram for central pattern generator for Sea Slug. I-inhibit, E-excite.

the tube feet of a predatory star fish, or by noxious chemical stimuli. When DSI fires a pulse burst it inhibits VSI, and excites C2. Then DSI and C2 fire together for a short period of time. While firing, VSI is being inhibited from DSI, but excited by C2. The inputs are summed, and VSI begins to fire, when threshold is reached VSI fires, inhibiting both DSI and C2, causing them to shut down. This shutdown of DSI and C2 decreases firing of VSI, completing a cycle. David Kleinfeld (1986), of AT&T Bell Laboratories, has built a central pattern generator with discrete components and operational amplifiers. The interested reader should consult his paper.

The next biological model I will discuss is the learning behavior of a garden slug, Limax maximus. This simple animal has been taught to avoid certain foods. The animal loves potatoes, this food preference is hardwired in its synaptic matrix. By spiking a potato with a bitter-tasting substance, the animal will learn to avoid potatoes. The experiment described by Gelperin et. al. (1985) is more elegant than this. Introducing the bitter tasting substance just before the animal takes a bite of the potato, adds a new dimension to the experiment. The animal must now learn to associate the taste of potatoes with the bitter-tasting material. In otherwords, a temporal element has been introduced into the experiment. This is not the same as the Hebb rule where synaptic weights are produced by simultaneous presynaptic and postsynaptic excitation. With this new learning rule there is a temporal delay between presynaptic and postsynaptic excitation.

OTHER LEARNING RULES

I would like to introduce, in a qualitative way, two other learning rules. The first learning rule is called *back propagation*. The network consists of three layers similar to Fig. 2-5. The input layer is connected to a hidden layer, which is connected to the output layer. A vector is sent through the input layers and it passes through the hidden layer to emerge at the output layer as the output vector. The difference in the actual output vector, and the desired output vector, is an error vector. This error vector is back propagated through the same network in reverse direction. The network will then adjust the weights to the error. After a few iterations the network will have learned the proper output response for a given input vector. Terrence Senjnouski (1986) has used this back propagation algorithm in a computer program called NETtalk. This computer simulation is connected to a pattern recognition, and speech synthesis system. The end result is that NETtalk can read English text out loud with a 95 percent performance level. The input layer is 29 neurons for the 26 letters in the alphabet, spaces, commas, and periods. The output layer consists of 26 units that encode phonenes and stresses, to drive the speech synthesizer. The middle layer is 60 neurons. Each input unit is connected to all 60 middle units and all 60 middle units are connected to the 26 output units. Each attempt at reading was compared with a phonetic transcription of a person reading the text. In a few hours NETtalk was able to read. This is a very impressive demonstration of the learning ability of neural networks.

The second learning rule I would like to discuss is a probability rule similar to a Boltzmann distribution. In Chapter 3, I introduced an energy relation given by:

$$E = -\tfrac{1}{2} \sum_{i=1}^{N} V_i^{t+1} \sum_{j=1}^{N} T_{ij} V_j^t$$

This relation can be written in a more compact form as:

$$E = -\tfrac{1}{2} \sum_{i \neq j} \sum T_{ij} V_i V_j$$

The change in E due to the change in V_i is given by:

$$\Delta E = -\Delta V_i \sum_{j \neq i} T_{ij} V_j$$

This is simply an energy gap. If the energy gap is positive, the neuron will turn on; otherwise, it will turn off. The probability that the neuron will assume a value of 1 is given by:

$$P_i = \frac{1}{1 + e^{-\Delta E/T}}$$

The term T, in this equation is called the annealing temperature. For large temperatures, P is about 0.5 and the neuron assumes a random state. For temperature equal to zero, the system behaves as a pure Hopfield network, moving down into the nearest local minimum. For any given temperature, the system will reach a thermal equilibrium. The probability of being in state A, versus a nearby state B, is given by the Boltzmann distribution:

$$\frac{P_A}{P_B} = e^{-(E_A - E_B)/T}$$

where E_A and E_B are the energies of states A and B.

The Boltzmann machine uses what is known as simulated annealing to escape from local minima. Simulated annealing consists of adding a random component to the decision process at each neuron, or threshold-logic unit. Boltzmann-machine learning consists of adjusting the weights of the network. The input units are clamped to an input pattern, and the network is annealed. The output pattern will appear on the output units. In a network that has learned, the output units will exhibit the same probability distribution, as if the network was still clamped.

A major advantage to the Boltzmann machine is that the laws of statistical thermodynamics can be applied to these networks, but only in a limited way. In bulk matter, where the laws of thermodynamics can apply, we are concerned with 10^{23} particles. Neural networks are not nearly that big.

FLOW-OF-ACTIVATION PROCESSING

I would like to introduce flow-of-activation processing. This is a building block principle for constructing artificial neural networks.

Cruz-Young (1986) and his associates have devised a massively parallel, non-von Neumann computing concept they call flow-of-activation networks (FAN). The FAN process is a massive artificial neural network. Each processor is called a node, and the communication paths are called links. These processors are simple threshold-logic devices, and the links are Hebbian synapses. Cruz-Young and coworkers at IBM have built a special hardware board for calculating the inner product of a matrix and a vector. The FAN is basically an abstraction of neural networks. The entire FAN system consists of a host computer, and the FAN coprocessor. A special compiler language called the General Network Language (GNL), was developed to make the system user-friendly.

The GNL compiler recognizes certain building blocks, such as items, ports, and links. The items are nodes or processors. The ports are input/output ports, to or from the network. The links are Hebbian connections. Cruz-Young and his associates have used this system for parallel collective computations such as optimization problems. In addition, they have used the system for robotic vision, and adaptive pattern-recognition. The boards are modular and can be interconnected with more FAN boards to make networks with up to one million processors, and 4 million links.

NEURAL NETWORK REFINEMENTS

There are other neural network models besides those already discussed. I will discuss a few other neural models. Heretofore, I have discussed a two-state model similar to Hopfield (1982). In Hopfield's later paper (1984), he discusses neurons with a graded response. The neuron saturates when the input u_i exceeds a threshold value. Figure 5-3 is a schematic for this model neuron. The relation for the charging of the amplifier is given by:

$$C_{si} \frac{du_i}{dt} = \sum_j T_{ij} V_j - \frac{u_i}{R_{si}} + I_i$$

and the charging time is given by:

$$\tau = RC_{si}$$

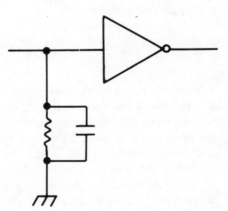

Fig. 5-3. Floating dendrite neuron model.

You could use operational amplifiers to build this network. Figure 5-4 shows a model neuron that has been designed for excitatory and inhibitory inputs. In the circuit of Fig. 5-4, V_i is the excitatory output and $-V_i$ is the inhibitory output from the neuron.

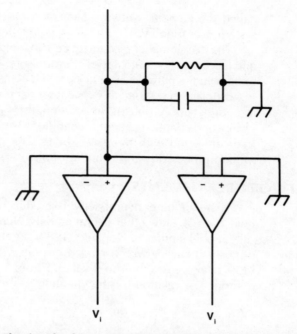

Fig. 5-4. Floating dendrite model with inhibitory and excitatory connections.

John Denker (1986) has introduced what he calls the virtual grounded neuron. Other models I have talked about are called floating dendrite. The circuit diagram for the virtual grounded neuron is given in Fig. 5-5, and the circuit equation is:

$$\sum_{j} (T_{ij}^{+} V_j - T_{ij}^{-} V_j) - C_i V_i - A^{-1} (V_i) = 0$$

In this relation u_i is the neuron input current. In the floating dendrite model u_i represented the input voltage. The transfer function A now represents transimpedance. In the floating dendrite model this function was voltage gain. The symbol T_{ij}^{+}, represents excitatory input and the symbol T_{ij}^{-}, represents inhibitatory conductance.

More complex "neural models" can be built. Batten (1987) has written an excellent text to discuss linear computational circuits. You could make neurons that compute derivatives or do integration, for example, from the ideas discussed in his book.

VLSI NEURAL NETWORKS

It is clear from the work in Chapter 4 that to build a very big artificial neural network would require a great deal of work. A network with N neurons

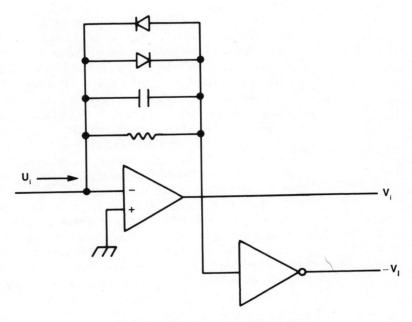

Fig. 5-5. Virtual grounded model neuron.

requires N^2 resistive interconnections. If each connection point could be addressed to program the network, it would require logic gates and more wires to each connection node. I do not wish to discourage experimentation on large networks; I, myself am building a 50-neuron circuit. I have seen some very impressive applications with small artificial neural networks. Networks with hundreds to millions of threshold processing units will require very large scale integration, perhaps wafer-scale integration. Some artificial intelligence laboratories are now doing research and development on medium scale integrated networks. In this section I will discuss some of that work.

Carver Mead (1987) of Caltech is doing some very impressive research and development on a vision chip, or an electronic retina. The lens of a vertebrate eye focuses an image on the surface of the retina, a tightly packed array of photo-receptors. The image produces signals that are transformed into nerve pulses that are transmitted over the optic nerve to higher brain centers. Mead's electronic retina contains a 48 × 48 array of phototransistors. The output of these phototransistors is sent to an array of analog processors. These processors do a lot more than act as threshold logic devices. They find logarithms, and derivatives, for example, just like the first level of processing in the back of the eye, before the data is sent on the optic nerve cable. Mead's electronic retina contains about 100,000 transistors in a total area of five millimeters by five millimeters. This is just a first step. The real beauty of artificial neural networks will come about with wafer scale integrated circuits.

These could easily contain billions of transistors. Neural networks are highly fault tolerant. Processors can be dead, and wires missing or not correctly connected, and the network will still work fine. You "burn out" thousands of neurons in your brain every day but you still function quite well. This is a result of parallel distributed processing with a fault tolerant system.

There has been several interesting VLSI circuits of artificial neural networks made at AT&T Bell Laboratories. Hubbard et. al. (1986) constructed a 22-neuron circuit. The connection matrix is a 22 × 22 resistor matrix built into a custom integrated circuit chip. The chip is, of course, pre-programmed for the stored vectors in the matrix. The 44-pin chip is plugged into a circuit board with CMOS inverters as neurons. The complete characterization of this chip is described in Hubbard's paper.

Hans Graf (1986) and coworkers at Bell Labs have constructed a 256-neuron circuit with a 256 × 256 resistor network on the same chip. The resistor matrix is a read-only matrix written by electron beam lithography. The chip includes two CMOS inverters for each neuron. One inverter each for inhibition and excitation. The chip also includes multiplexing lines for communications. The entire chip is 5.7mm × 5.7mm in area.

Another project at AT&T Bell Laboratories involves a 52-neuron, fully programmable neural network chip. The chip, described by Graf and deVegon (1987), is a CMOS chip with about 75,000 transistors. Each cross point in the 52 × 52 matrix can be addressed with software. The chip includes inhibitory and excitatory connections. Researchers at Bell Laboratories have used the chip to study associative memories and sequence analyzer circuits.

Thakoor (1987), at the Jet Propulsion Laboratory, has been experimenting with electronically programmable resistor networks. The matrix consists of a thin layer of resistive material sandwiched between two sets of very fine wires. The best material tested has been amorphous semiconducting films such as silicon and germanium. These resistor networks would be read-only networks and would be written with electronic pulses.

APPLICATIONS

A few applications of neural networks other than content-addressable memories are demonstration devices that have been built at various laboratories to serve as examples.

The first application I will discuss is analog-to-digital conversion. Like many problems that neural networks solve, this is an optimization problem. The neural network must compare an analog signal to a reference signal, and decide what the unknown signal level is, then convert from analog to digital representation. Tank and Hopfield (1986) have constructed a four-bit A/D converter. The connection matrix consists of resistors of increasing value, as shown in Fig. 5-6. These matrix elements are conductances.

The reference signal must be fed into the amplifiers and the analog signal must be injected into the amplifiers in proportion to the input value of the

$$\begin{bmatrix} 0 & 2 & 4 & 8 \\ 2 & 0 & 8 & 16 \\ 4 & 8 & 0 & 32 \\ 8 & 16 & 32 & 0 \end{bmatrix}$$

Fig. 5-6. Conductance matrix for A/D converter.

analog signal. For example, a row of conductances such as (1 2 4 8) will serve for injecting the analog signal. So the analog and reference signal could be injected into the matrix as shown in Fig. 5-7.

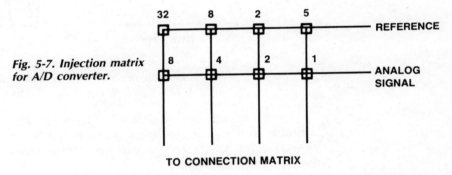

Fig. 5-7. Injection matrix for A/D converter.

In Fig. 5-7 the connections are given as conductances. Results of running this circuit have an appearance similar to that sketched in Fig. 5-8. Notice this is not a smooth A/D conversion.

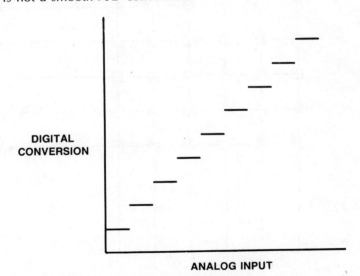

Fig. 5-8. Schematic of I/O relationship for neural A/D converter.

Another application is signal decomposition. This is clearly an optimization decision problem. This problem has also been discussed by Tank and Hopfield (1986). If you are given a signal similar to that shown in Fig. 5-9A, it can be decomposed to a signal similar to that shown in Fig. 5-9B.

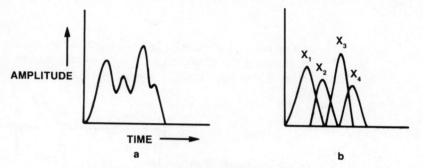

**Fig. 5-9. Example of signal decomposition problem.
A. raw signal. B. decomposed signal.**

The neural network circuit used to analyze and decompose this signal is similar to the analog-to-digital conversion case. In this case, there is a network of resistors before the synapse resistor network. Figure 5-10 shows the presynaptic network.

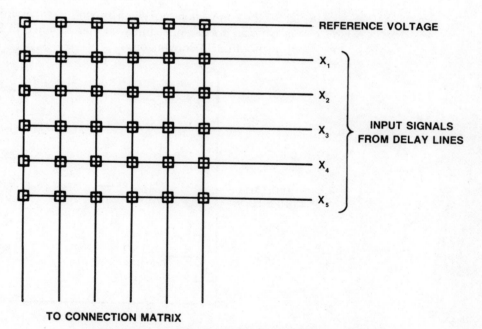

Fig. 5-10. Preconnection matrix for signal optimization problem.

This type of circuit could be used in speech recognition because speech signals are similar to those represented in Fig. 5-9.

I would like to mention a few other applications in passing. Pattern recognition is obvious. I also pointed out in the section on biological models that David Kleinfeld (1986) has built a central pattern generator circuit with discrete components. As a final application I would like to mention that Babcock and Westervelt (1986) and Maxwell, et. al. (1986) have described nonlinear oscillator circuits from neural networks. These were digital computer simulations and appear to be an open field for the experimenter.

CORPORATIONS IN NEURAL NETWORKING

There are a number of corporations involved in neural networking. I have already mentioned extensive projects at AT&T Bell Laboratories, Caltech, Jet Propulsion Laboratories, and IBM. This section is an annotated list of corporations. All prices quoted are at time of writing.

Texas Instruments

Texas Instruments is selling a LISP-based workstation to run a coprocessor board for neural network simulations. The Odyssey board is selling for $12,500 and the workstation for $28,000.

Hecht-Nielsen Neurocomputer

A new start-up company in San Diego, Hecht-Nielsen Neurocomputer, is offering the ANZA neurocomputer. This is a coprocessor-board compatible with the IBM PC/AT host and runs MS-DOS. The system will simulate 30,000 neurons and 300,000 interconnections. The ANZA board sells for $9500.

Science Applications International

Science Applications International in La Jolla, CA is offering a coprocessor board for the IBM PC/AT at $25,000. It simulates a million neurons.

Neural Systems Inc.

Neural Systems Inc., Vancouver, British Columbia, is doing contract work for Caltech's Jet Propulsion Laboratory to develop a neural system for robotic arm control. Their primary business is building custom boards as coprocessors. They also offer a $2000 expert system that uses neural network principles.

Nestor

Nestor, Providence, RI, is offering a $1600, IBM PC program to recognize handwritten information on insurance forms and other documents.

FUTURE TECHNOLOGIES: BEYOND THE FIFTH GENERATION —————

This section discusses several advanced technologies that hold some promise for computers of the future. We will first look at technologies that are currently under development, and then move into more speculative technologies that we will not see before the 21st Century, or later.

GaAs Chips

The first advanced technology I will discuss is gallium arsenide (GaAs) chips. In GaAs the effective mass of the electron is only about seven percent of what it is in silicon. This means that the GaAs electron mobility is about five to seven times faster than the silicon electron mobility. So the GaAs chips can operate about five times faster for the same or lower power requirements. GaAs chips are excellent for microwave circuits, LEDs, and lasers. The possibility exists of integrating the lasers, and electronics, on a single chip. This could result in telecommunication repeaters being directly connected to fiber optic cables. Much higher-speed data communication would thus be possible.

Other major advantages of GaAs are higher radiation resistance, and a wider working temperature range. The silicon chips can withstand 10^3 to 10^4 rads of radiation and GaAs chips can withstand 10^7 to 10^8 rads. The working temperature range is -200 to $+200$ degrees Celsius, and by special processing, GaAs chips can be made to run as hot as 300 to 400 degrees Celsius. Although the military would be very happy to have these chips, space scientists would also be happy. Gallium arsenide chips would be a good choice for space probes and robots used to operate in a harsh environment.

Optical Computers

The next future technology I'd like to discuss is optical computing. It is possible to construct a hybrid computer with pn junctions that are used to stimulate and detect light. The GaAs materials discussed would be a good first choice. An optical computer must be purely optical since any hybrid approach will suffer from the limitations of an electronics interface.

One approach to an all optical computer is an optical NOR gate array, which can be constructed in the following manner. Two checkerboard images are projected on a common surface to give an OR resulting image. After inverting in contrast and threshold the intensity is the NOR of the inputs. The output of these NOR gates is used as the inputs of other NOR gates. The interconnection is performed with a hologram. The reference point source (X,Y) is associated with three object point sources at $(X,Y-1)$, $(X+1,Y-1)$, and $(X+2,Y-1)$. Such a distribution system would distribute the outputs of any number of inputs in parallel.

An interesting recent development by Abraham, et. al. (1983), is a device known as a transphasor, the optical analog of the transistor. The transphasor uses what is known as nonlinear optical materials. Just as a transistor operates by an electrical signal switching another signal, the transphasor operates by a laser beam switching another laser beam. This is a major breakthrough in optical computing. Applications with this device should be very interesting.

An optical neural computer could be constructed from an input array and an output array. The input array would generate optical signals such as laser pulses. The input array could be a bistable optical device, a transphasor, or pn diodes with associated electronics. The interconnection matrix could be a volume hologram such as a photorefractive crystal. A photorefractive crystal generates free charges that can be trapped in a pattern by an incoming laser beam. The spatially varying charge density that results creates internal fields that change the index of refraction within the crystal and produce the 3-D hologram. This will require years of research until a computer can be built that operates like this.

Josephson Junctions

A Josephson Junction operates by electron tunneling. Two strips of superconducting material are separated by an insulating layer such as an oxide. When cooled to near liquid helium temperature, -270 degrees Celsius, a superconducting electron can tunnel across the junction. A magnetic field generated by a nearby circuit is able to switch the Josephson junction between on and off states. This device can be used as a logic element in a computer. Recent breakthroughs in superconducting materials have resulted in superconductivity at -180 degrees Celsius about 20 degrees above liquid nitrogen.

The new materials research began to explode in late 1986, when Bednorz and Muller at IBM discovered superconductivity in lanthanum barium copper oxide. This discovery lead to the obvious substitution of strontium for barium. I said obvious because strontium and barium are in the same group in the periodic table of the elements. The lanthanum strontium copper oxide was reported by Kishio, et. al. (1987), at the University of Tokyo and by workers at AT&T Bell Labs. Another obvious substitution by Wu, et. al (1987), lead to the discovery of yttrium barium copper oxide. This material has the highest confirmed superconducting transition temperature at -180 degrees Celsius. These new breakthroughs in materials will add new life to Josephson junction computing research.

Molecular Electronic Devices

A very exciting possibility is molecular-scale computing elements. Forrest Carter (1982, 1983) envisions computers constructed from molecular logic elements. Molecules known as charge transfer complexes, such as TTF-TCNQ, can be used as diodes. Conducting polymers, such as polysulfurnitride, can be used as molecular wires. Photoactive molecules can transmit a signal after receiving a photon of light. Certain molecular groups can be used to recognize other groups. Information storage is possible in complex polymers such as DNA and proteins. Molecular recognition and assembly is also possible. Proteins and enzymes are used to assemble complex structures, such as living organisms and biocomputers. Ulmer (1983) has suggested using genetic engineering to modify bacteria to grow molecular electronic devices, and Drexler (1986) has suggested a whole nanotechnology of molecular-scale machines.

In conclusion, we can look forward to some fascinating scientific and technological breakthroughs in the twenty-first Century. Many of these technologies can be applied to artificial neural network research.

Appendices

A

Final Run of the Four Interpenetrating Flip-Flop Experiments

The following table is the complete print out from the four interpenetrating flip-flop experiment described in Chapter 4.

0	0 0 0 0 0 0 0 0
170	1 0 1 0 1 0 1 0
1	0 0 0 0 0 0 0 1
170	1 0 1 0 1 0 1 0
2	0 0 0 0 0 0 1 0
105	0 1 1 0 1 0 0 1
3	0 0 0 0 0 0 1 1
232	1 1 1 0 1 0 0 0
4	0 0 0 0 0 1 0 0
170	1 0 1 0 1 0 1 0
5	0 0 0 0 0 1 0 1
170	1 0 1 0 1 0 1 0
6	0 0 0 0 0 1 1 0
105	0 1 1 0 1 0 0 1

7	0 0 0 0 0 1 1 1
232	1 1 1 0 1 0 0 0
8	0 0 0 0 1 0 0 0
178	1 0 1 1 0 0 1 0
9	0 0 0 0 1 0 0 1
150	1 0 0 1 0 1 1 0
10	0 0 0 0 1 0 1 0
113	0 1 1 1 0 0 0 1
11	0 0 0 0 1 0 1 1
212	1 1 0 1 0 1 0 0
12	0 0 0 0 1 1 0 0
178	1 0 1 1 0 0 1 0
13	0 0 0 0 1 1 0 1
178	1 0 1 1 0 0 1 0
14	0 0 0 0 1 1 1 0
113	0 1 1 1 0 0 0 1
15	0 0 0 0 1 1 1 1
240	1 1 1 1 0 0 0 0
16	0 0 0 1 0 0 0 0
170	1 0 1 0 1 0 1 0
17	0 0 0 1 0 0 0 1
142	1 0 0 0 1 1 1 0
18	0 0 0 1 0 0 1 0
105	0 1 1 0 1 0 0 1
19	0 0 0 1 0 0 1 1
204	1 1 0 0 1 1 0 0
20	0 0 0 1 0 1 0 0
170	1 0 1 0 1 0 1 0
21	0 0 0 1 0 1 0 1
170	1 0 1 0 1 0 1 0

22   0 0 0 1 0 1 1 0
105   0 1 1 0 1 0 0 1

23   0 0 0 1 0 1 1 1
232   1 1 1 0 1 0 0 0

24   0 0 0 1 1 0 0 0
178   1 0 1 1 0 0 1 0

25   0 0 0 1 1 0 0 1
178   1 0 1 1 0 0 1 0

26   0 0 0 1 1 0 1 0
113   0 1 1 1 0 0 0 1

27   0 0 0 1 1 0 1 1
240   1 1 1 1 0 0 0 0

28   0 0 0 1 1 1 0 0
178   1 0 1 1 0 0 1 0

29   0 0 0 1 1 1 0 1
178   1 0 1 1 0 0 1 0

30   0 0 0 1 1 1 1 0
113   0 1 1 1 0 0 0 1

31   0 0 0 1 1 1 1 1
240   1 1 1 1 0 0 0 0

32   0 0 1 0 0 0 0 0
142   1 0 0 0 1 1 1 0

33   0 0 1 0 0 0 0 1
142   1 0 0 0 1 1 1 0

34   0 0 1 0 0 0 1 0
77   0 1 0 0 1 1 0 1

35   0 0 1 0 0 0 1 1
204   1 1 0 0 1 1 0 0

36   0 0 1 0 0 1 0 0
170   1 0 1 0 1 0 1 0

37	0 0 1 0 0 1 0 1
170	1 0 1 0 1 0 1 0
38	0 0 1 0 0 1 1 0
105	0 1 1 0 1 0 0 1
39	0 0 1 0 0 1 1 1
232	1 1 1 0 1 0 0 0
40	0 0 1 0 1 0 0 0
150	1 0 0 1 0 1 1 0
41	0 0 1 0 1 0 0 1
150	1 0 0 1 0 1 1 0
42	0 0 1 0 1 0 1 0
85	0 1 0 1 0 1 0 1
43	0 0 1 0 1 0 1 1
212	1 1 0 1 0 1 0 0
44	0 0 1 0 1 1 0 0
178	1 0 1 1 0 0 1 0
45	0 0 1 0 1 1 0 1
178	1 0 1 1 0 0 1 0
46	0 0 1 0 1 1 1 0
113	0 1 1 1 0 0 0 1
47	0 0 1 0 1 1 1 1
240	1 1 1 1 0 0 0 0
48	0 0 1 1 0 0 0 0
142	1 0 0 0 1 1 1 0
49	0 0 1 1 0 0 0 1
142	1 0 0 0 1 1 1 0
50	0 0 1 1 0 0 1 0
77	0 1 0 0 1 1 0 1
51	0 0 1 1 0 0 1 1
204	1 1 0 0 1 1 0 0

52	0 0 1 1 0 1 0 0
170	1 0 1 0 1 0 1 0
53	0 0 1 1 0 1 0 1
170	1 0 1 0 1 0 1 0
54	0 0 1 1 0 1 1 0
105	0 1 1 0 1 0 0 1
55	0 0 1 1 0 1 1 1
232	1 1 1 0 1 0 0 0
56	0 0 1 1 1 0 0 0
150	1 0 0 1 0 1 1 0
57	0 0 1 1 1 0 0 1
150	1 0 0 1 0 1 1 0
58	0 0 1 1 1 0 1 0
85	0 1 0 1 0 1 0 1
59	0 0 1 1 1 0 1 1
212	1 1 0 1 0 1 0 0
60	0 0 1 1 1 1 0 0
178	1 0 1 1 0 0 1 0
61	0 0 1 1 1 1 0 1
178	1 0 1 1 0 0 1 0
62	0 0 1 1 1 1 1 0
113	0 1 1 1 0 0 0 1
63	0 0 1 1 1 1 1 1
240	1 1 1 1 0 0 0 0
64	0 1 0 0 0 0 0 0
43	0 0 1 0 1 0 1 1
65	0 1 0 0 0 0 0 1
142	1 0 0 0 1 1 1 0
66	0 1 0 0 0 0 1 0
43	0 0 1 0 1 0 1 1

| 67 | 0 1 0 0 0 0 1 1 |
| 170 | 1 0 1 0 1 0 1 0 |

| 68 | 0 1 0 0 0 1 0 0 |
| 43 | 0 0 1 0 1 0 1 1 |

| 69 | 0 1 0 0 0 1 0 1 |
| 170 | 1 0 1 0 1 0 1 0 |

| 70 | 0 1 0 0 0 1 1 0 |
| 43 | 0 0 1 0 1 0 1 1 |

| 71 | 0 1 0 0 0 1 1 1 |
| 170 | 1 0 1 0 1 0 1 0 |

| 72 | 0 1 0 0 1 0 0 0 |
| 51 | 0 0 1 1 0 0 1 1 |

| 73 | 0 1 0 0 1 0 0 1 |
| 150 | 1 0 0 1 0 1 1 0 |

| 74 | 0 1 0 0 1 0 1 0 |
| 51 | 0 0 1 1 0 0 1 1 |

| 75 | 0 1 0 0 1 0 1 1 |
| 178 | 1 0 1 1 0 0 1 0 |

| 76 | 0 1 0 0 1 1 0 0 |
| 51 | 0 0 1 1 0 0 1 1 |

| 77 | 0 1 0 0 1 1 0 1 |
| 178 | 1 0 1 1 0 0 1 0 |

| 78 | 0 1 0 0 1 1 1 0 |
| 51 | 0 0 1 1 0 0 1 1 |

| 79 | 0 1 0 0 1 1 1 1 |
| 178 | 1 0 1 1 0 0 1 0 |

| 80 | 0 1 0 1 0 0 0 0 |
| 43 | 0 0 1 0 1 0 1 1 |

| 81 | 0 1 0 1 0 0 0 1 |
| 142 | 1 0 0 0 1 1 1 0 |

```
82        0 1 0 1 0 0 1 0
43        0 0 1 0 1 0 1 1

83        0 1 0 1 0 0 1 1
170       1 0 1 0 1 0 1 0

84        0 1 0 1 0 1 0 0
43        0 0 1 0 1 0 1 1

85        0 1 0 1 0 1 0 1
170       1 0 1 0 1 0 1 0

86        0 1 0 1 0 1 1 0
43        0 0 1 0 1 0 1 1

87        0 1 0 1 0 1 1 1
170       1 0 1 0 1 0 1 0

88        0 1 0 1 1 0 0 0
51        0 0 1 1 0 0 1 1

89        0 1 0 1 1 0 0 1
178       1 0 1 1 0 0 1 0

90        0 1 0 1 1 0 1 0
51        0 0 1 1 0 0 1 1

91        0 1 0 1 1 0 1 1
178       1 0 1 1 0 0 1 0

92        0 1 0 1 1 1 0 0
51        0 0 1 1 0 0 1 1

93        0 1 0 1 1 1 0 1
178       1 0 1 1 0 0 1 0

94        0 1 0 1 1 1 1 0
51        0 0 1 1 0 0 1 1

95        0 1 0 1 1 1 1 1
178       1 0 1 1 0 0 1 0

96        0 1 1 0 0 0 0 0
15        0 0 0 0 1 1 1 1
```

| 97 | 0 1 1 0 0 0 0 1 |
| 142 | 1 0 0 0 1 1 1 0 |

| 98 | 0 1 1 0 0 0 1 0 |
| 15 | 0 0 0 0 1 1 1 1 |

| 99 | 0 1 1 0 0 0 1 1 |
| 142 | 1 0 0 0 1 1 1 0 |

| 100 | 0 1 1 0 0 1 0 0 |
| 43 | 0 0 1 0 1 0 1 1 |

| 101 | 0 1 1 0 0 1 0 1 |
| 170 | 1 0 1 0 1 0 1 0 |

| 102 | 0 1 1 0 0 1 1 0 |
| 43 | 0 0 1 0 1 0 1 1 |

| 103 | 0 1 1 0 0 1 1 1 |
| 170 | 1 0 1 0 1 0 1 0 |

| 104 | 0 1 1 0 1 0 0 0 |
| 23 | 0 0 0 1 0 1 1 1 |

| 105 | 0 1 1 0 1 0 0 1 |
| 150 | 1 0 0 1 0 1 1 0 |

| 106 | 0 1 1 0 1 0 1 0 |
| 23 | 0 0 0 1 0 1 1 1 |

| 107 | 0 1 1 0 1 0 1 1 |
| 150 | 1 0 0 1 0 1 1 0 |

| 108 | 0 1 1 0 1 1 0 0 |
| 51 | 0 0 1 1 0 0 1 1 |

| 109 | 0 1 1 0 1 1 0 1 |
| 178 | 1 0 1 1 0 0 1 0 |

| 110 | 0 1 1 0 1 1 1 0 |
| 51 | 0 0 1 1 0 0 1 1 |

| 111 | 0 1 1 0 1 1 1 1 |
| 178 | 1 0 1 1 0 0 1 0 |

```
112     0 1 1 1 0 0 0 0
15      0 0 0 0 1 1 1 1

113     0 1 1 1 0 0 0 1
142     1 0 0 0 1 1 1 0

114     0 1 1 1 0 0 1 0
15      0 0 0 0 1 1 1 1

115     0 1 1 1 0 0 1 1
142     1 0 0 0 1 1 1 0

116     0 1 1 1 0 1 0 0
43      0 0 1 0 1 0 1 1

117     0 1 1 1 0 1 0 1
170     1 0 1 0 1 0 1 0

118     0 1 1 1 0 1 1 0
43      0 0 1 0 1 0 1 1

119     0 1 1 1 0 1 1 1
170     1 0 1 0 1 0 1 0

120     0 1 1 1 1 0 0 0
23      0 0 0 1 0 1 1 1

121     0 1 1 1 1 0 0 1
150     1 0 0 1 0 1 1 0

122     0 1 1 1 1 0 1 0
23      0 0 0 1 0 1 1 1

123     0 1 1 1 1 0 1 1
150     1 0 0 1 0 1 1 0

124     0 1 1 1 1 1 0 0
51      0 0 1 1 0 0 1 1

125     0 1 1 1 1 1 0 1
178     1 0 1 1 0 0 1 0

126     0 1 1 1 1 1 1 0
51      0 0 1 1 0 0 1 1
```

127	0 1 1 1 1 1 1 1
178	1 0 1 1 0 0 1 0
128	1 0 0 0 0 0 0 0
43	0 0 1 0 1 0 1 1
129	1 0 0 0 0 0 0 1
142	1 0 0 0 1 1 1 0
130	1 0 0 0 0 0 1 0
105	0 1 1 0 1 0 0 1
131	1 0 0 0 0 0 1 1
77	0 1 0 0 1 1 0 1
132	1 0 0 0 0 1 0 0
43	0 0 1 0 1 0 1 1
133	1 0 0 0 0 1 0 1
43	0 0 1 0 1 0 1 1
134	1 0 0 0 0 1 1 0
105	0 1 1 0 1 0 0 1
135	1 0 0 0 0 1 1 1
105	0 1 1 0 1 0 0 1
136	1 0 0 0 1 0 0 0
23	0 0 0 1 0 1 1 1
137	1 0 0 0 1 0 0 1
150	1 0 0 1 0 1 1 0
138	1 0 0 0 1 0 1 0
85	0 1 0 1 0 1 0 1
139	1 0 0 0 1 0 1 1
85	0 1 0 1 0 1 0 1
140	1 0 0 0 1 1 0 0
51	0 0 1 1 0 0 1 1
141	1 0 0 0 1 1 0 1
51	0 0 1 1 0 0 1 1

```
142      1 0 0 0 1 1 1 0
113      0 1 1 1 0 0 0 1

143      1 0 0 0 1 1 1 1
113      0 1 1 1 0 0 0 1

144      1 0 0 1 0 0 0 0
15       0 0 0 0 1 1 1 1

145      1 0 0 1 0 0 0 1
142      1 0 0 0 1 1 1 0

146      1 0 0 1 0 0 1 0
105      0 1 1 0 1 0 0 1

147      1 0 0 1 0 0 1 1
77       0 1 0 0 1 1 0 1

148      1 0 0 1 0 1 0 0
43       0 0 1 0 1 0 1 1

149      1 0 0 1 0 1 0 1
43       0 0 1 0 1 0 1 1

150      1 0 0 1 0 1 1 0
105      0 1 1 0 1 0 0 1

151      1 0 0 1 0 1 1 1
105      0 1 1 0 1 0 0 1

152      1 0 0 1 1 0 0 0
51       0 0 1 1 0 0 1 1

153      1 0 0 1 1 0 0 1
178      1 0 1 1 0 0 1 0

154      1 0 0 1 1 0 1 0
113      0 1 1 1 0 0 0 1

155      1 0 0 1 1 0 1 1
113      0 1 1 1 0 0 0 1

156      1 0 0 1 1 1 0 0
51       0 0 1 1 0 0 1 1
```

157   1 0 0 1 1 1 0 1
51   0 0 1 1 0 0 1 1

158   1 0 0 1 1 1 1 0
113   0 1 1 1 0 0 0 1

159   1 0 0 1 1 1 1 1
113   0 1 1 1 0 0 0 1

160   1 0 1 0 0 0 0 0
15   0 0 0 0 1 1 1 1

161   1 0 1 0 0 0 0 1
15   0 0 0 0 1 1 1 1

162   1 0 1 0 0 0 1 0
77   0 1 0 0 1 1 0 1

163   1 0 1 0 0 0 1 1
77   0 1 0 0 1 1 0 1

164   1 0 1 0 0 1 0 0
43   0 0 1 0 1 0 1 1

165   1 0 1 0 0 1 0 1
43   0 0 1 0 1 0 1 1

166   1 0 1 0 0 1 1 0
105   0 1 1 0 1 0 0 1

167   1 0 1 0 0 1 1 1
105   0 1 1 0 1 0 0 1

168   1 0 1 0 1 0 0 0
23   0 0 0 1 0 1 1 1

169   1 0 1 0 1 0 0 1
23   0 0 0 1 0 1 1 1

170   1 0 1 0 1 0 1 0
85   0 1 0 1 0 1 0 1

171   1 0 1 0 1 0 1 1
85   0 1 0 1 0 1 0 1

| 172 | 1 0 1 0 1 1 0 0 |
| 51 | 0 0 1 1 0 0 1 1 |

| 173 | 1 0 1 0 1 1 0 1 |
| 51 | 0 0 1 1 0 0 1 1 |

| 174 | 1 0 1 0 1 1 1 0 |
| 113 | 0 1 1 1 0 0 0 1 |

| 175 | 1 0 1 0 1 1 1 1 |
| 113 | 0 1 1 1 0 0 0 1 |

| 176 | 1 0 1 1 0 0 0 0 |
| 15 | 0 0 0 0 1 1 1 1 |

| 177 | 1 0 1 1 0 0 0 1 |
| 15 | 0 0 0 0 1 1 1 1 |

| 178 | 1 0 1 1 0 0 1 0 |
| 77 | 0 1 0 0 1 1 0 1 |

| 179 | 1 0 1 1 0 0 1 1 |
| 77 | 0 1 0 0 1 1 0 1 |

| 180 | 1 0 1 1 0 1 0 0 |
| 43 | 0 0 1 0 1 0 1 1 |

| 181 | 1 0 1 1 0 1 0 1 |
| 105 | 0 1 1 0 1 0 0 1 |

| 182 | 1 0 1 1 0 1 1 0 |
| 105 | 0 1 1 0 1 0 0 1 |

| 183 | 1 0 1 1 0 1 1 1 |
| 105 | 0 1 1 0 1 0 0 1 |

| 184 | 1 0 1 1 1 0 0 0 |
| 23 | 0 0 0 1 0 1 1 1 |

| 185 | 1 0 1 1 1 0 0 1 |
| 23 | 0 0 0 1 0 1 1 1 |

| 186 | 1 0 1 1 1 0 1 0 |
| 85 | 0 1 0 1 0 1 0 1 |

187   1 0 1 1 1 0 1 1
85   0 1 0 1 0 1 0 1

188   1 0 1 1 1 1 0 0
51   0 0 1 1 0 0 1 1

189   1 0 1 1 1 1 0 1
113   0 1 1 1 0 0 0 1

190   1 0 1 1 1 1 1 0
113   0 1 1 1 0 0 0 1

191   1 0 1 1 1 1 1 1
113   0 1 1 1 0 0 0 1

192   1 1 0 0 0 0 0 0
43   0 0 1 0 1 0 1 1

193   1 1 0 0 0 0 0 1
15   0 0 0 0 1 1 1 1

194   1 1 0 0 0 0 1 0
43   0 0 1 0 1 0 1 1

195   1 1 0 0 0 0 1 1
43   0 0 1 0 1 0 1 1

196   1 1 0 0 0 1 0 0
43   0 0 1 0 1 0 1 1

197   1 1 0 0 0 1 0 1
43   0 0 1 0 1 0 1 1

198   1 1 0 0 0 1 1 0
43   0 0 1 0 1 0 1 1

199   1 1 0 0 0 1 1 1
43   0 0 1 0 1 0 1 1

200   1 1 0 0 1 0 0 0
23   0 0 0 1 0 1 1 1

201   1 1 0 0 1 0 0 1
23   0 0 0 1 0 1 1 1

```
202     1 1 0 0 1 0 1 0
51      0 0 1 1 0 0 1 1

203     1 1 0 0 1 0 1 1
51      0 0 1 1 0 0 1 1

204     1 1 0 0 1 1 0 0
51      0 0 1 1 0 0 1 1

205     1 1 0 0 1 1 0 1
51      0 0 1 1 0 0 1 1

206     1 1 0 0 1 1 1 0
51      0 0 1 1 0 0 1 1

207     1 1 0 0 1 1 1 1
51      0 0 1 1 0 0 1 1

208     1 1 0 1 0 0 0 0
15      0 0 0 0 1 1 1 1

209     1 1 0 1 0 0 0 1
15      0 0 0 0 1 1 1 1

210     1 1 0 1 0 0 1 0
43      0 0 1 0 1 0 1 1

211     1 1 0 1 0 0 1 1
43      0 0 1 0 1 0 1 1

212     1 1 0 1 0 1 0 0
43      0 0 1 0 1 0 1 1

213     1 1 0 1 0 1 0 1
43      0 0 1 0 1 0 1 1

214     1 1 0 1 0 1 1 0
43      0 0 1 0 1 0 1 1

215     1 1 0 1 0 1 1 1
43      0 0 1 0 1 0 1 1

216     1 1 0 1 1 0 0 0
51      0 0 1 1 0 0 1 1
```

217   1 1 0 1 1 0 0 1
51   0 0 1 1 0 0 1 1

218   1 1 0 1 1 0 1 0
51   0 0 1 1 0 0 1 1

219   1 1 0 1 1 0 1 1
51   0 0 1 1 0 0 1 1

220   1 1 0 1 1 1 0 0
51   0 0 1 1 0 0 1 1

221   1 1 0 1 1 1 0 1
51   0 0 1 1 0 0 1 1

222   1 1 0 1 1 1 1 0
51   0 0 1 1 0 0 1 1

223   1 1 0 1 1 1 1 1
51   0 0 1 1 0 0 1 1

224   1 1 1 0 0 0 0 0
15   0 0 0 0 1 1 1 1

225   1 1 1 0 0 0 0 1
15   0 0 0 0 1 1 1 1

226   1 1 1 0 0 0 1 0
15   0 0 0 0 1 1 1 1

227   1 1 1 0 0 0 1 1
15   0 0 0 0 1 1 1 1

228   1 1 1 0 0 1 0 0
43   0 0 1 0 1 0 1 1

229   1 1 1 0 0 1 0 1
43   0 0 1 0 1 0 1 1

230   1 1 1 0 0 1 1 0
43   0 0 1 0 1 0 1 1

231   1 1 1 0 0 1 1 1
43   0 0 1 0 1 0 1 1

| 232 | 1 1 1 0 1 0 0 0 |
| 23 | 0 0 0 1 0 1 1 1 |

| 233 | 1 1 1 0 1 0 0 1 |
| 23 | 0 0 0 1 0 1 1 1 |

| 234 | 1 1 1 0 1 0 1 0 |
| 23 | 0 0 0 1 0 1 1 1 |

| 235 | 1 1 1 0 1 0 1 1 |
| 23 | 0 0 0 1 0 1 1 1 |

| 236 | 1 1 1 0 1 1 0 0 |
| 51 | 0 0 1 1 0 0 1 1 |

| 237 | 1 1 1 0 1 1 0 1 |
| 51 | 0 0 1 1 0 0 1 1 |

| 238 | 1 1 1 0 1 1 1 0 |
| 51 | 0 0 1 1 0 0 1 1 |

| 239 | 1 1 1 0 1 1 1 1 |
| 51 | 0 0 1 1 0 0 1 1 |

| 240 | 1 1 1 1 0 0 0 0 |
| 15 | 0 0 0 0 1 1 1 1 |

| 241 | 1 1 1 1 0 0 0 1 |
| 15 | 0 0 0 0 1 1 1 1 |

| 242 | 1 1 1 1 0 0 1 0 |
| 15 | 0 0 0 0 1 1 1 1 |

| 243 | 1 1 1 1 0 0 1 1 |
| 15 | 0 0 0 0 1 1 1 1 |

| 244 | 1 1 1 1 0 1 0 0 |
| 43 | 0 0 1 0 1 0 1 1 |

| 245 | 1 1 1 1 0 1 0 1 |
| 43 | 0 0 1 0 1 0 1 1 |

| 246 | 1 1 1 1 0 1 1 0 |
| 43 | 0 0 1 0 1 0 1 1 |

| 247 | 1 1 1 1 0 1 1 1 |
| 43 | 0 0 1 0 1 0 1 1 |

| 248 | 1 1 1 1 1 0 0 0 |
| 23 | 0 0 0 1 0 1 1 1 |

| 249 | 1 1 1 1 1 0 0 1 |
| 23 | 0 0 0 1 0 1 1 1 |

| 250 | 1 1 1 1 1 0 1 0 |
| 23 | 0 0 0 1 0 1 1 1 |

| 251 | 1 1 1 1 1 0 1 1 |
| 23 | 0 0 0 1 0 1 1 1 |

| 252 | 1 1 1 1 1 1 0 0 |
| 51 | 0 0 1 1 0 0 1 1 |

| 253 | 1 1 1 1 1 1 0 1 |
| 51 | 0 0 1 1 0 0 1 1 |

| 254 | 1 1 1 1 1 1 1 0 |
| 51 | 0 0 1 1 0 0 1 1 |

| 255 | 1 1 1 1 1 1 1 1 |
| 51 | 0 0 1 1 0 0 1 1 |

B

Decimal, Hexadecimal, and Binary Equivalents

Decimal	Hex	Binary
0	0	0000
1	1	0001
2	2	0010
3	3	0011
4	4	0100
5	5	0101
6	6	0110
7	7	0111
8	8	1000
9	9	1001
10	A	1010
11	B	1011
12	C	1100
13	D	1101
14	E	1110
15	F	1111

References

Abraham, E., Seaton, C., and Smith, D., *Scientific American*, Feb., 1983

Abraham, R.H., and Shaw, C.D., Dynamics-The Geometry of Behavior, *Part 2: Chaotic Behavior*, Aerial Press, 1985

Babcock, K.L., and Westervelt, R.M., "Neural Networks for Computing," edited by Denker, J.S., *American Institute Proceedings* #151. Snowbird, UT 1986

Batten, G.L., *Design and Application of Linear Computational Circuits*, TAB Professional and Reference Books, 1987

Bednorz, J.G., and Müller, K.A., *Zurich fuer Physiks*, B64 (1986)

Bennett, C.H., IBM *Journal of Research & Development*, 6, 525, (1979)

Bernstein, J., *Three Degrees Above Zero: Bell Labs in the Information Age*, Mentor New American Library, 1984

Carter, F.L., *Molecular Electronic Devices*, Marcel Dekker, 1982

Carter, F.L., *Computer Applications in Chemistry*, edited by Heller and Potenzone, Elsevier Science Publishers, 1983

Cruz-Young, C.A., "Neural Networks for Computing," *American Institute of Physics* #151

Denker, J.S., *Physica*, 22D, 216-232, (1986)

Denker, J.S., "Neural Networks for Computing," *American Institute of Physics* #151

deVegvor, P.G.N., and Graf, H.P., *Workshop on Neural Network Devices and Applications*, Jet Propulsion Lab., Feb., 1987

Drexler, K.E., *Engines of Creation*, Doubleday, 1986

Fredkin, E., and Toffoli, T., *International Journal of Theoretical Physics*, 21, p219, 1982

Gelperin, A., Hopfield, J.J., and Tank, D.W., *Model Neural Networks and Behavior*, edited by Silverston, A.I., Plenum Press, 1985

Getting, P.A., and Dekin, M.S., *Model Neural Networks and Behavior*, edited by Silverston, A.I., Plenum Press, 1985

Goldsbrough, P.F., *Microcomputer Interfacing with the 8255 PPI Chip*, Howard W. Sams & Co., 1980

Graf, et. al., "Neural Networks for Computing," *American Institute of Physics* #151

Hebb, D.O., *The Organization of Behavior*, Wiley, 1949

Hillis, W.D., *The Connection Machine*, MIT Press, 1985

Hopfield, J.J., *Proc. Natl. Acad. Sci. USA*, 79, 2554-2558, 1982

Hopfield, J.J., *Proc. Natl. Acad. Sci. USA*, 81 3088-3092, 1984

Hubbard, et. al., "Neural Networks for Computing," *AIP* #151

Kishio, Kitazawa, Kanbe, Yasuda, Sugii, Takagi, Uchida, Fueki, and Tanaka, Chem. Lett. 429 (1987); Cava, van Dover, Batlogg, Rietman, *Phys. Rev. Lett.* 58, 408 (1987)

Kleinfeld, D., Proceeding National Academy of Science *USA*, 83, 9469-9473, 1986

Kohonen, T., *Self-Organization and Associative Memory*, Springer-Verlag, 1984

Maxwell, et. al., "Neural Networks for Computing," *AIP* #151

McEliece, R.J., Posner, E.C., and Rodemich, E.R., *Twenty Third Annual Allerton Conference on Communication, Control and Computing*, Oct., 1985

Mead, C., *Engineering and Science*, Published at Caltech, June 1987

Mims, F.M. III, *Engineer's Notebook II*, Radio Shack #276-5002 (1982)

Rumelhart, D.E., McClelland, J.L., and the PDP Research Group, "Parallel Distributed Processing: Explorations in the Microstructure of Cognation," *Volume I: Foundations*, MIT Press 1986

Sejnouski and Rosenberg, *paper presented at the Eighth Annual Conference of the Cognition Society*, Aug., 1986

Tank, D.W. and Hopfield, J.J., *IEEESystems Trans. Circuits and Systems* CAS33 (5) 533-541, 1986

Thakoor, A.P., "Content-Addressable High Density Memories Based on Neural Network Models," *Jet Propulsion Laboratory Report* #JPLD-4166, (1987)

Ulmer, K.M., *Molecular Electronic Devices*, edited by Forrest Carter, Marcel Dekker, 1982

von Neumann, J., *Theory of Self-Reproducing Automata*, Univ. of Illinois Press, 1966

Wu, Ashburn, Tory, Hor, Meny, Gao, Huang, Wang, Chu, *Physics Review Letter*, 58, 908, (1987)

Annotated Bibliography

Books and Conference Proceedings

Denker, J.S. (Editor, 1986). "Neural Networks For Computing," *AIP Conference Proceedings #151*, American Institute of Physics.
    (This is the first published conference proceedings that discusses artificial neural networks at some length.)

Parallel Distributed Processing, Rumelhart, D.E., McClelland, J.L. and the PDP Research Group (1986)., MIT Press.
    (This work is in two volumes. The first volume concerns the foundations of parallel distributed processing and the second concerns psychological and biological models.)

Self-Organization and Associative Memory, Kohonen, T. (1984). Springer-Verlag.
    (This is an advanced book and requires a fair degree of mathematical understanding.)

"Workshop on Neural Network Devices and Applications (1987)," *Jet Propulsion Laboratory*, February 18 and 19, 1987.
    (This workshop proceedings is a printed copy of viewgraphs presented.)

The Organization of Behavior, Hebb, D.O. (1949)., Wiley.
    (This is the original work of Hebb, where he published his ideas of learning at the synaptic level.)

Model Neural Networks and Behavior, Silverston, A.I. (editor, 1985)., Plenum Press.
 (A very biology oriented book.)

Applied Optics (September 15, 1986 and May 15, 1987).
 (These two special issues of Applied Optics are devoted to optical computing and includes many articles on optical neural computing.)

The Computer and the Brain, Ladd, S. (1986), Bantam Books.
 (A laymans account of advanced computers. Includes neural networks.)

Content-Addressable Memories, Kohonen, T. (1987), Springer-Verlag.
 (This is a revised second edition of an earlier work. Requires a good mathematical understanding.)

The Society of Mind, Minsky, M. (1986), Simon and Schuster.
 (This is a layman account of the network theory of the mind and brain.)

Biological Information Processing: Current Theory and Computer Simulation, Sampson, J.R. (1984), Wiley.
 (This textbook covers advanced algorithms.)

Bienenstock, E., Fogelman Soulie, F. and Weisbuch, G. (editors 1986). "Disordered Systems and Biological Organization," *Springer-Verlag.*
 (This is the conference proceedings of a NATO workshop on disordered systems held in March 1985.)

Farmer, D., Lapedes, A., Packard, N. and Wendroff, B. (editors 1986). "Evolution, Games and Learning: Models for Adaptation in Machines and Nature," North-Holland Amsterdam.
 (This conference proceedings was published in a special issue of *Physica D,* vol. 22D, October-November 1986. It is the proceedings of the Fifth Annual International Conference of the Center for Nonlinear Studies Los Alamos, NM, May 20-24, 1985.)

Journal Articles and Papers

Lambe, J., Thakoor, A.P., and Moopenn, A. (November 15, 1985). "Content-Addressable, High-Density Memories Based on Neural Network Models," *Technical Progress Report* #JPL D-2825, Jet Propulsion Laboratory, Pasadena, California.
 (This is a very readable paper that includes the theroy of neural networks and a discussion of a small neural network the authors built.)

Thakoor, A.P.. "Content-Addressable, High Density Memories Based on Neural Network Models," (March 1987), *Technical Progress Report* #JPL D-4166, Jet Propulsion Laboratory.

Brown, R.J.. *Dr. Dobb's Journal of Software Tools,* 12 (4), 16-27, April 1987.
    (This article on neural networks includes a computer program in C. The algorithm is a back propagation.)

Larson, E.. "Neural Chips," OMNI, 113, November 1986.

Bear, M.F., Copper, L.N. and Ebner, F.F. "A Physiological Basis for a Theory of Synapse Modification," *Science,* 237 42-47, July 3, 1987.

Rosenblatt, F. "The Percepron A Perceiving and Recognizing Automation," (1957) *Cornell Aeronautical Laboratory Report #85-460-1.*
    (One of the first papers to discuss an artificial neural network.)

Kleinfeld, D. and Tank, D.W. "Control of Neuronal-Substratum Adhesion Using Surface Modification and Photolithographic Techniques," *Biophysical Journal,* (1986) 49 P233a.
    (This is a technique for culture of neural cells on IC's.)

Crill, W.E. and Schwindt, P.C.. "Active Currents in Mammalian Central Neurons," *TINS,* 236-240 June 1983.

Anninos, P.A.. "The Usefulness of Artificial Neural Nets as Models for the Normal and Abnormal Functioning of the Mammalian CNS," *Progress in Neurobiology* (1975) 4 57-78.

Personnaz, L., Guyon, I. and Dreyfus, G.. "Collective Computational Properties of Neural Networks: New Learning Mechanisms," *Physical Review* A 34(5) 4217-4228 November 1986.
    (A new method of plotting state space is introduced here.)

Kirkpatrick, S., Gelatt, C.D. and Vecchi, M.P.. "Optimization by Simulated Annealing," *Science* 220 4598 671-680 May 13, 1983.
    (A technique related to the Boltzmann Machine.)

Rosenfeld, E.. Intelligence: The Future of Computing. (*A news letter published by E. Rosenfeld,* P.O. Box 20008, New York, NY 10025.)

McElaece, R.J., Posner, E.C., and Rodemich, E.R.. "A Preliminary Analysis of the Hopfield Associative Memory" 23-rd *Annual Allerton Conference on Communication, Control and Computing,* October 1985.

(This paper concerns the signal-to-noise ratio in content-addressable memories.)

Hopfield, J.J. and Tank, D.W.. "Computing with Neural Circuits: A Model," *Science* 233 625-633 August 8, 1986.
(This paper is a summary of other papers by Hopfield and Tank.)

Hopfield, J.J.. "Neural Networks and Physical Systems With Emergent Collective Computational Abilities" *Proc. Natl. Acad. Sci.* USA 79 2554-2558, April 1982.
(This is Hopfield's first paper on neural networks. An understanding of this paper is a must for neural networkers.)

Hopfield, J.J.. "Neurons With Graded Response Have Collective Computational Properties Like Those of Two-State Neurons," *Proc. Natl. Acad. Sci.* USA 81 3088-3092, May 1984.
(This is Hopfield's second paper and should also be read.)

Chester, M.. "Dress Rehearsal for Real-Time Artificial Neural Networks," *Electronic Products*, 19-28, June 15, 1987.
(This article describes some of the products to be on display at the IEEE conference on neural networks held in June 1987, in San Diego.)

Port, O. and Wilson, J.W.. "They're Here: Computers That 'Think'," Science and Technology section in *Business Week*, 94-98, January 26, 1987.
(This article discusses some of the start-up companies in neural networks.)

Kinoshita, J. and Palevsky, N.G.. "Computing With Neural Networks," *High Technology* 24-31 May 1987.
(This is a lay article which includes a list of the companies in neural networks.)

Research & Development, "Research into Neural Networks of the Brain Could Advance Associative Memory for Computers" *Research and Development*, February 1986.
(This article is based on an interview with Hopfield and discusses the possibility of using neural networks to advance computers.)

Chester, M.. "The Military Reconnoiters Neural Systems," *Electronic Products*, p78-81 October 15, 1986.
(This article discusses the military applications for neural networks.)

Tank, D.W. and Hopfield, J.J.. "Simple Neural Optimization Networks: An A/D Converter, Signal Decision Circuit, and a Linear Programming Circuit,"

IEEE Transactions on Circuits and Systems, CAS-33,5, p533-541, May 1985.
(Advanced descriptions of some artificial neural network circuits.)

Kleinfeld, D. (1988). "Sequential State Generation by Model Neural Networks," *Proc. Natl. Acad. Sci. USA,* 83 p9469-9473, December 1986.
(This paper requires good mathematical understanding.)

Gray, R.M.. "Vector Quantization," *IEEE ASSP Magazine,* p4-29, April 1984.
(Vector quantization can be used to map complex images for neural network pattern recognation systems.)

Fahlman, S.E. and Hinton, G.E.. "Connectionist Architectures for Artificial Intelligence," *IEEE Computer,* p100-109, January 1987.
(A good introduction to connectionist architectures.)

Rosenberg, C.R. and Sejnowski, T.J.. "The Spacing Effect on NETtalk, A Massively-Parallel Network" *Cognitive Science Laboratory Report #2 Princeton University.*
(This is a paper presented at the Eighth Annual Conference of the Cognitive Science Society held at Amherst, Massachusetts, August 1986.)

Kleinfeld, D.. "A Simple Neural Network That Exhibits Associative Memory: A Model of Four Neurons."
(Report from an informal lecture sponsored by the Neural Systems and Behavior Course, *Marine Biological Laboratory,* July 26, 1984.)

Little, W.A.. "The Existance of Persistent States in the Brain," *Mathematical Biosciences* 19, 101-120, 1974.
(An early paper in which an analogy is drawn between the persistant states in the brain and Ising spin systems, such as spin glasses.)

Harth, E.. "Order and Chaos in Neural Systems: An Approach to the Dynamics of Higher Brain Functions," *IEEE Transactions on Systems, Man, and Cybernetics,* SMC-13, 5, p782-789, October 1983.
(Describes neural dynamics, pattern generation and chaos.)

Thompson, J.M.. "Dynamical Field Theories for Neural Activity in the Brain," *Instabilities and Catastrophes in Science and Engineering,* Wiley (1982).
(An excellent book for an introduction to chaotic dynamics.)

van Hemmen, J.L. and Kuhn, R.. "Nonlinear Neural Networks," *Physical Review Letters,* 57, 7 p913-916, August 18, 1986.
(An advanced mathematical paper.)

Scott, A.C.. "Neurodynamics: A Critical Survey," *Journal of Mathematical Psychology* 15, (1977) p1-45.

Koch, C., Marroquin, J. and Yuille, A., "Analog Neural Networks in Early Vision," *Proc. Natl. Acad. Sci.* USA, 83 p4263-4267, June 1986.
   (Discusses concepts such as edge detection and motion analysis.)

Shrager, J., Hogg, T. and Huberman, B.A.. "Observation of Phase Transitions in Spreading Activation Networks," *Science,* 236, p1092-1094, May 29, 1987.
   (These concepts are used in Boltzman machine analysis.)

Rumelhart, D.E., Hinton, G.E. and Williams, R.J.. "Learning Representations by Back-Propagating Errors" *Nature,* 323, p533-536, October 9, 1986.

Palm, G.. "On Associative Memory," *Biological Cybernetics,* 36, (1980) p19-31.
   (The storage capacity and usefulness of associative memories are discussed.)

Hopfield, J.J., Feinstein, D.I. and Palmer, R.G.. "Unlearning Has A Stabilizing Effect in Collective Memories" *Nature* 304, p158-159, July 14, 1983.
   (This is similar to the principle that reducing the synaptic strength can increase storage capacity of the neural network.)

Kohonen, T., Lehtio, P., Rovamo, J., Hyvarinen, J., Bry, K. and Vainio, L.. "A Principle of Neural Associative Memory," *Neuroscience,* 2, (1977) p1065-1076.
   (An early paper in associative memory theory.)

Thakoor, A.P., Lamb, J.L., Moopenn, A. and Khanna, S.K.. "Binary Synaptic Connections Based on Memory Switching in a-Si:H for Artificial Neural Networks" *Jet Propulsion Laboratory.*
   (Paper presented at the Materials Research Society Meeting, Anaheim, April 1987.)

Anderson, J.A., Silverstein, J.W., Ritz, S.A. and Jones, R.S.. "Distinctive Features, Categorical Perception, and Probability Learning: Some Applications of a Neural Model," *Psychological Review* 84 (5) p413-451, September 1977.
   (A hybrid model, partly analog and partly binary, is presented for learning.)

McCulloch, W.S. and Pitts, W.. "A Logical Calculus of the Ideas Immanent in Nervous Activity," *Bulletin of Mathematical Biophysics* 5, (1943) p115-133.
   (This is the first paper on neural network theory.)

Wilson, H.R. and Cowan, J.D.. "Excitatory and Inhibitory Interactions in Localized Populations of Model Neurons" *Biophysical Journal* 12, p1-24, 1972.
(This paper developes a system of nonlinear differential equations to describe the dynamics of model neurons.)

Conrad, M.. "Limits on the Computing Power of Biological Systems," *Bulletin of Mathematical Biology* 43, p59-67, 1981.
(This paper shows that a parallelism allows polynomial time algorithms to be used more efficiently.)

Conrad, M.. "Microscopic-Macroscopic Interface in Biological Information Processing," *Biosystems* 16, p345-363, 1984.
(A number of models are briefly sketched which illustrate how molecular switching processes could be recruited for useful biological functions.)

Nodes, T.A., Smith, J.L. and Hecht-Nielsen, R.. "A Fuzzy Associative Memory Module and its Application to Signal Processing." *IEEE*, (1985) CH2118-8/85/0000-1511.
(This paper describes an associative memory device. Hecht-Nielsen is the founder of HNC Neurocomputer Corporation in San Diego.)

Crisanti, A., Amit, D.J. and Gutfreund, H.. "Saturation Level of the Hopfield Model for Neural Network," *Europhysics Letters* 2 (4), p337-341, August 15, 1986.
(This paper requires advanced mathematics for understanding it.)

Jeffrey, W. and Rosner, R.. "Optimization Algorithms: Simulated Annealing and Neural Network Processing," *Astrophysical Journal*, 310, (1986) p473-481, November 1, 1986.
(Requires advanced math.)

Personnaz, L., Guyon, I. and Dreyfus, G.. "Information Storage and Retrieval in Spin-Glass like Neural Networks," *J. Physique Letters* 46 L359-L365, April 15, 1985.

Peretto, P.. "Collective Properties of Neural Networks: A Statistical Physics Approach," *Biological Cybernetics* 50, p51-62, 1984.
(A statistical physics approach is used to study the dynamics of neural networks. This paper requires an advanced understanding of math.)

Cohen, M.A. and Grossberg, S.. "Absolute Stability of Global Pattern Formation and Parallel Memory Storage by Competitive Neural Networks,"

IEEE Transactions on Systems, Man and Cybernetics SMC-13 (5), p815-826, September/October 1983.

(This article discusses pattern formation in neural networks, and shows that chaos does not result. This article requires advanced mathematics.)

Amit, D.J., Gutfreund, H.. and Sompolinsky, H. "Storing Infinite Numbers of Patterns in a Spin-Glass Model of Neural Networks," *Physical Review Letters* 55 (14), p1530-1533, September 30, 1985.

(The paper shows that the number of patterns that can be stored is about 0.14*N, where N is the number of neurons.)

Anderson, J.A.. "Cognitive and Psychological Computation with Neural Models," *IEEE Transactions on Systems, Man and Cybernetics*, SMC-13 (5), p799-815, September/October 1983.

Hameroff, S.R. and Watt, R.C.. "Information Processing in Microtubules," *J. Theoretical Biology* 98, p549-561, (1982).

(An information processing model is developed in which microtubules play a major part. Microtubules are polymerized cytoskeletal proteins.)

Conrad, M.. "Molecular Information Structures in the Brain," *Journal of Neuroscience Research* 2, p233-254, (1976).

(The paper presents a theory of memory and learning based on the manipulation of macromolecular conformations.)

Fredkin, E. and Toffoli, T.. "Conservative Logic," *International Journal of Theoretical Physics*, 21 (3/4) p219-253 (1982).

(This paper developes the ideas of conserved information processing as found with the *controlled* NOT gate.)

Kohonen, T.. "An Adaptive Associative Memory Principle," *IEEE Transactions on Computers*, p444-445, April 1974.

(An early paper on associative memory.)

Liberman, Y.A., Minina, S.V., and Golubtsov, K.V.. "Study of the Metabolic Synapse - I. Effect of Intracellular Micro Injection of 3′, 5′-AMP" *Biophysics* 20 (3), p451-456 1975.

(A very biology oriented article.)

Conrad, M.. "Information Processing in Molecular Systems" *Currents in Modern Biology* 5, (1972) p1-14.

(Molecular self-reproducing systems process information in a hierarchical mode, based on the fact of hierarchy in molecular structure.)

Liberman, Y.A., Minina, S.V. and Shklovskii, N.Y.. "Depolarization of the Neural Membrane on Exposure to Cyclic 3′, 5′-Adenosine Monophosphate and its Possible Role in the Work of the Molecular Computer of the Neuron" *Biophysics* 23, p308-314, 1978.

Kampfner, R.R. and Conrad, M.. "Computational Modeling of Evolutionary Learning Processes in the Brain." *Bulletin of Mathematical Biology* 45 (6), (1983) p931-968.

Kampfner, R.R. and Conrad, M.. "Sequential Behavior and Stability Properties of Enzymatic Neuron Networks" *Bulletin of Mathematical Biology* 45 (6), (1983) p969-980.

Index

Index

Other Bestsellers of Related Interest

BUILD YOUR OWN UNIVERSAL COMPUTER INTERFACE—Bruce Chubb

With this practical ideas and step-by-step building instruction presented in this book, you can construct the electronic interfacing circuits needed to use your microcomputer to control all types of external devices. Here are the technology and the hands-on application examples you need to set up a general-purpose computer interface that is easily attachable to over 100 computers. 320 pages, 224 illustrations. Book No. 3122, $19.95 paperback, $27.95 hardcover

THE FIFTH GENERATION: The Future of Computer Technology—Jeffrey Hsu and Joseph Kusnan

The *Fifth Generation* presents a clear, readable account of applications, research, and technologies that make up the fifth generation. Authors Hsu and Kusnan cover each aspect of the subject in depth including: fifth-generation research, parallel processing, microchip technologies, speech processing, vision systems, robotics, programming languages, natural language and expert systems. 208 pages, 30 illustrations. Book No. 3069, $16.95 paperback, $26.95 hardcover

THE HANDBOOK OF MICROCOMPUTER INTERFACING—2nd Edition—Steve Leibson

"It contains a wealth of information needed by anyone working closely with microcomputers."—**BYTE** magazine

Offering practical insight and use-it-now information on every aspect of interfacing, Leibson covers hardware, software, and the history and theory of interfacing practices. You'll learn how to: attach perpherals from any manufacturer—even homebuilt units . . . and use your computer to control everything from household appliances to amateur radio equipment. 336 pages, 268 illustrations. Book No. 3101, $19.95 paperback, $29.95 hardcover

MASTER HANDBOOK OF MICROCOMPUTER LANGUAGES—2nd Edition—Charles F. Taylor, Jr.

This detailed edition is an overview of computer languages, specifically high-level languages, that are available for use on microcomputers. A general description and discussion of what a *high-level language* is, what it does, and what it can and cannot do, it followed by a thorough examination of each of the following languages: BASIC, LISP, PILOT, Prolog, Ada, Fortran, COBOL, Logo, Pascal, C, Modula-2, and Forth. 508 pages, 215 illustrations. Book No. 2893, $17.95 paperback, $26.95 hardcover

EXPERIENCING ARTIFICIAL INTELLIGENCE: An Interactive Approach for the Apple®—John J. Monroe and Mark R. Hilbush

Just like having a personal instructor, this disk-based tutorial carries you through the process of learning about artificial intelligence techniques by letting you see and experience them on your Apple screen. To make this book easier to understand, corresponding software has been included. The disk includes an interactive set of chapters that follow those in the books and clearly illustrates the concepts as they are described. Book plus 3 Disks for Apple *II* with 64K, Apple DOS 3.3 and 80-column card, 492 pages, 116 illustrations. Book No. 2860, $36.95 paperback only

CHIP TALK: PROJECTS IN SPEECH SYNTHESIS—Dave Prochnow

Now you can explore speech synthesis easily and inexpensively with the help of this excellent introduction. Includes step-by-step instructions for constructing a variety of working synthesizers—both stand-alone and computer-interfaced units—at a fraction of the cost of comparable commercial units. Also, included: BASIC programs that will enable you to interface with the Apple® II, the Macintosh®, and the Commodore 64™/128™. 224 pages, 131 illustrations. Book No. 2812, $14.95 paperback, $24.95 hardcover

THE POWER OF TURBO PROLOG: THE NATURAL LANGUAGE OF ARTIFICIAL INTELLIGENCE—Ralph Roberts

The newest development in artificial intelligence and expert systems programming is Turbo Prolog—a powerful, super-fast Prolog computer from Borland International that gives IBM PC, AT, and compatible users programming options previously available only with the latest, most powerful mainframe computers. For the thousands who have invested in Turbo Prolog, or plan to, this is the comprehensive guide. 208 pages, 77 illustrations. Book No. 2782, $14.95 paperback, $22.95 Hardcover

EXPERT SYSTEMS: A NON-PROGRAMMERS GUIDE TO DEVELOPMENT AND APPLICATIONS—Paul Siegel

This exceptional guide opens the way to a tremendous range of applications for expert systems that you can use in your everyday business. It clarifies how to implement a system, including ways to define problems. You'll learn what an expert system is, methods of thinking that will help you in problem solving, simplified rule language, machine reasoning, and more! 256 pages, 108 illustrations. Book No. 2738, $29.95 hardcover only

EXPERT SYSTEMS FOR MICROCOMPUTERS— An Introduction to Artificial Intelligence—Michael Chadwick and John Hannah

Here, you'll find all the programming techniques needed to put "intelligence" into your microcomputer using BASIC or Logo . . . to create expert system programs that accomplish exactly what you want them to for any business or personal purpose. Leading off with an introduction to expert systems, the authors explain the principles of rule-based systems and demonstrate practical applications. 240 pages, 90 illustrations. Book No. 2838, $14.95 paperback, $19.95 hardcover

HE ROBOT BUILDER'S BONANZA: 99 INEXPENSIVE ROBOTICS PROJECTS—Gordon McComb and John Cook

Where others might only see useless surplus parts you can imagine a new "life form." Now, there's a book that will help you make your ideas and dreams a reality. With the help of the *Robot Builder's Bonanza* you can truly express your creativity. This fascinating guide offers you a complete, unique collection of tested and proven project modules that you can mix and match to create an almost endless variety of highly intelligent and workable robot creatures. 336 pages, 283 illustrations. Book No. 2800, $14.95 paperback, $23.95 hardcover

BUILD YOUR OWN WORKING ROBOT—THE SECOND GENERATION—David L. Heiserman

Are you bored with ordinary, every-day types of electronic projects? Ready for a real challenge? Meet Buster . . . an amazing, personal robot that you can build yourself. You'll get instructions on the two modes Buster operates under—his independent one in which he uses his blunder response to run freely without operator control . . . and dependent mode in which he is in the control of the person using the Operator's Control Panel. 140 pages, 37 illustrations. Book No. 2781, $12.95 paperback, $18.95 hardcover

DESIGNING AND PROGRAMMING PERSONAL EXPERT SYSTEMS—Carl Townsend and Dennis Feucht

Discover how new trends in artificial intelligence (AI) concepts can be put to practical use on almost any personal computer including Apple® II or IBM® PC! Explore expert system programming techniques to create your own system for electronics, engineering, or other technical applications! It's all here for the taking in this exciting and challenging new sourcebook! 250 pages, 75 illustrations. Book No. 2692, $18.95 paperback, $27.95 hardcover

ARTIFICIAL INTELLIGENCE: Theory, Logic and Application—James F. Brule

Explore the leading edge of computer technology . . . probe the outer limits of business productivity offered by today's new-generation microcomputers . . . discover the real-world business applications potential offered by artificial intelligence (AI) techniques! Covers the potentials, the alternatives, and practical advantages and disadvantages of expert systems and AI as business tools. 192 pages, 35 illustrations. Book No. 2671, $12.95 paperback only

HANDBOOK OF ADVANCED ROBOTICS—Edward L. Safford, Jr.

Here's your key to learning how today's sophisticated robot machines operate, how they are controlled, what they can do, and how you can put this modern technology to work in a variety of applications. Plus, you'll find complete instructions for building your own remote-controlled hobby robot, get a detailed look at available commercial robots and androids, and gain an understanding of today's different types of robot machines. 480 pages, 242 illustrations. Book No. 1421, $16.50 paperback only

THE COMPUTER SECURITY HANDBOOK—Richard H. Baker

Electronic breaking and entering into computers systems used by business, industry and personal computerists has reached epidemic proportions This up-to-date sourcebook provides a realistic examination of today's computer security problems, shows you how to analyze your home and business security needs, and gives you guidance in planning your own computer security system. 288 pages, 61 illustrations. Book No. 2608, $32.95 hardcover only

HOW TO DESIGN AND BUILD YOUR OWN CUSTOM ROBOT—David L. Heiserman

Now, you can have a robot that "thinks" and "reacts" like you want it to! This incredible, up-to-the-minute sourcebook provides every bit of data you need to make that robot a reality, right in your own home workshop! All the procedures for planning, putting together, and programming a custom-designed parabot, and even an Alpha- or Beta-Class robot are included in this exciting guide to robotics! 462 pages, 247 illustrations. Book No. 1341, $14.95 paperback only

---

Look for These and Other TAB Books at Your Local BOOKSTORE

To Order Call Toll Free 1-800-822-8158

(in PA and AK call 717-794-2191)

or write to TAB BOOKS Inc., Blue Ridge Summit, PA 17294-0840.

Title	Product No.	Quantity	Price

☐ Check or money order made payable to TAB BOOKS Inc.

Charge my ☐ VISA ☐ MasterCard ☐ American Express

Acct. No. _____ Exp. _____

Signature: _____

Name: _____

City: _____

State: _____ Zip: _____

Subtotal $ _____

Postage and Handling
($3.00 in U.S., $5.00 outside U.S.) $ _____

In PA, NY, & ME add
applicable sales tax $ _____

TOTAL $ _____

TAB BOOKS catalog free with purchase; otherwise send $1.00 in check or money order and receive $1.00 credit on your next purchase.

Orders outside U.S. must pay with international money order in U.S. dollars.

TAB Guarantee: If for any reason you are not satisfied with the book(s) you order, simply return it (them) within 15 days and receive a full refund. BC